Mommy's Inspirations

Weekly Devotional & Journal for Mothers of Young Children

By Krystal Torres

Cover designed with Canva

Krystal Torres
Visit my website at www.treesofhope.net

Printed in the United States of America

First Printing: April 2018
Kindle Direct Publishing

ISBN-9781980936350

Contents

Special thanks:

My copy editor Shannon Welty
Photographer Rodney Herrera Escandon

I dedicate this book to:

My loving parents, Hope and Dale, who nurtured and encouraged us as children to seek and follow Christ always in our lives.

My devoted and faithful husband Jorge Luis, who has shown me grace in my times of weakness and loved me still.

My beautiful children Cielo (in heaven), Luke, Bennett, Laurelle, and Davin. From all of you I have grown more deeply into the knowledge and love of Christ.

My incredible siblings Amber, Brittany, and Jared. So glad we are family!

All my "mommy friends" and other moms out there who are doing motherhood on a daily basis. You are not alone!

My One and only Jesus, who has loved me when I have felt unlovable. My gratitude for Your great love and mercy is unending.

INTRODUCTION

I am a daughter, a sister, a friend, a wife, and now a mother. Motherhood has truly been a mix of unique experiences, in which such purpose and joy is met with times of extreme challenge and character development. It has forever changed me, and continues to do so. Please know that Jesus is at work in motherhood, if we can surrender this rewarding task to Him first!

The writings in this book were birthed out of my own profound appreciation for God's great gift of little miracles. It was written over the course of a year, and is designed to be read week by week, although you are welcome to read one a day. The short scripture verses and simple weekly applications are intentional for us as women and mothers. The journal pages are there to leave a record of your own reflections for each week. I trust it will be a source of guidance, as you allow Christ to shape you into the mother He has created you to be.

May you sincerely seek Jesus throughout this year, receiving His grace when you fail (as we all do and will), and come out a braver and more confident mother and woman of God for the world to behold. God bless you!

∞ ∞ ∞

1. Weakness Turns into Strength

*A*s I write this entry, I feel exhausted! I could say I feel this way at the end of most days, but today especially I couldn't think of a better adjective than that to encapsulate the essence of my feelings.

When we as mothers feel this way, the predominant way of thinking is that we are unable to function and be useful. This may be true enough, for if the exhaustion you are experiencing is total exhaustion, you will need to force yourself to stop, nap, or ask for help from someone else so you can rest (even if it hurts your pride).

Yet, the other side of the coin is that when we are weak, the Bible reminds us that HE is strong. Weakness is something our world rejects, yet Christ embraced. Without Him becoming weak and broken, literally, we would not have the hope of glory, which is Christ living in us and giving us true, abundant life and purpose on earth.

The most beautiful moms that I know are weak. They can admit that there are trials in their marriage, in their walk with the Lord, and in the day-to-day responsibilities of being a mommy. These are the people I want to surround myself with. Why? Not because it makes me feel superior, although I have to guard myself so that I am not tempted to think so. I surround myself with women like this because it clues me in to my own reality of imperfection and weakness. Once we admit this, we have won half the battle. The "other half" always has to be surrendered at the cross, where we confess to God that we cannot do anything on our own, but plead for His power to be unleashed into our broken lives.

Jesus, I need to remind myself that feeling weak is not a bad thing. Give me the ability to embrace my weakness, and enjoy watching YOU take over.

Scripture of the week:

2 Corinthians 12:9-10

But he said to me, "My grace is sufficient for you, for my power is made perfect in weakness." Therefore, I will boast all the more gladly about my weaknesses, so that Christ's power may rest on me. That is why, for Christ's sake, I delight in weaknesses, in insults, in hardships, in persecutions, in difficulties. For when I am weak, then I am strong.

Practical Weekly Application:

1. Spend time reading *The Bible* and in prayer with God.
2. Reflect on the weaknesses in your life as a mother, wife, etc., and then list how God's work has overcome those areas. Pray for Jesus to remind you that He is your strength.

Weakness Turns into Strength

2. Sitting in the Judgment Seat?

I caught myself. It was a gorgeous sunny day and we were out at a nearby park. A black car pulled up with tinted windows and stopped abruptly as a little girl, around four or five years old, got out. With a pink baby binky in her mouth, she moseyed on over to the area where my boys and I were playing. Her mother stood outside of her car to watch from a distance while lighting her cigarette and talking on the phone. A million thoughts raced through my mind. I wasn't looking for an opportunity to reach out; I was looking down on this mother and attempting to distance myself.

No one enjoys being negatively judged by others. I think one of the worst feelings comes when another mother decides that she knows better than you, and tries to impose her way over yours. Yet, how often do these same thoughts of judgment enter into our own hearts and minds when we see a fellow mom who is "less than perfect" in our shallow estimation? Let us stop this losing battle before it ever begins!

Formula versus breast milk, cloth versus disposable diapers, homemade versus store-bought food, hand-me-downs versus the latest trends in clothing, and the list goes on. Why would we be tempted to judge another mom in the first place? When I contemplate that question, I realize we're insecure and uncertain as mothers and want to prove to ourselves that our way is right and that we are good moms.

Motherhood requires so much of us. It is a constant and never-ending responsibility that follows us no matter where we are, and no matter how old our children become. We will always be their mommy. Let's use our energy, words, and time to build one another up and partner together as mamas. Reach out to the moms who seem to be struggling, as we too are works in progress as well by the mighty Hand of God alone.

The mission we are all on, raising our children, is a common one, so let's become allies rather than adversaries on this grand adventure. Uniting together in our common goals and aspirations is much better than focusing on the divisiveness of personal choices and opinions that each mother will make based on her own experience, abilities, circumstances, and preferences. Let go of the judgmental spirit in you. Learn from those moms who differ from you, and find the common ground as young moms who want the best for their children.

Jesus, cut out the judgmental and critical spirit that seeks to overtake my thoughts and heart. I desire to see the needs of others that go deeper than the differences I may be inclined to focus on. Give me Your compassionate heart and wise understanding towards mothers and others in general.

Scripture of the Week

Romans 14:13
Therefore, let us stop passing judgment on one another. Instead, make up your mind not to put any stumbling block or obstacle in the way of a brother or sister.

Practical Weekly Application:

1. Spend time reading *The Bible* and in prayer with God.
2. Pray over the fellow mothers in your life. Contact at least one friend or family member who is a mother this week and talk specifically about this issue. Perhaps it is or will be someone who varies comparatively in her approach to motherhood. Pray together that God would help each of you in this area.

Sitting in the Judgment Seat?

3. Goodbye My Love

On April 28, 2010, I received the horrific news that our first little baby, still inside my womb, had passed away. She was only 12 weeks old at the time, but to me she was already so alive. Even as I write this I am welling up with tears, as I know this little life was taken straight up to heaven, though selfishly I would have loved to have met her first here. One day.

Tragedy strikes us. I have spoken with friends who have lost children and read autobiographies and memoirs of moms that have gone through terrible losses. Yet, when it happens to you, it is as if the world stops.

The grieving process for me was more than I would have expected. I vividly remember having numerous panic attacks over the next few months. I felt guilty. Somehow I was the one who was unfit to carry this child and properly bring her into the world, right? No. Believing such a lie for too long would have been detrimental. What I came to accept is something we may all know but don't want to fully embrace: God allowed this to happen, and I simply don't understand it now and maybe never will.

As young moms, there are many questions that are constantly going through our heads on a given day. For example, "What should I feed the kids today?" or "What time should I put them to bed tonight? Am I a present enough mother? Can I get a shower at some point? Am I teaching them enough about Christ through my example? Will I regret something when they're all grown up?" Some of these questions are more easily answered, but others may be questions that persist in our minds for a long time, or forever. The mom who has to stop breastfeeding despite the desire to continue, or another who has to go back to work for a time although emotionally she is not ready. How can we be okay with this? If we believe that our Heavenly Father loves US, then we can have confidence and know that we, as HIS daughters, are being taken care of and are in the best hands: His.

You aren't the only one taking care of you and your children, and therefore you don't have to carry guilt and shame for every challenge and circumstance that comes your way. When I dealt with my own miscarriage, I had to let the tears of disappointment intertwine with the knowledge of Jesus's presence: He was still with me, had a plan even for this, and was there to help me cope with the pain and bring hope to my distress.

Thank you, Jesus, for being my best friend and sweet Savior. Even when I feel alone, remind me that You care for me and think of me often.

Scripture of the Week

John 10:14-15

"I am the good shepherd; I know my sheep and my sheep know me— just as the Father knows me and I know the Father—and I lay down my life for the sheep."

Practical Weekly Application:

1. Spend time in *The Bible* and in prayer with God.
2. Write a letter to Your Heavenly Father this week. Pour out your heart and tell Him how much you desire to trust that you are constantly being cared for by Him. It can be short, long, specific, or general, but make sure it is sincere and heartfelt above all.

Goodbye My Love

4. "Mama Right Here"

The current age range of my boys is just so precious, although I have said that at every stage so far! It is a refreshing time to see their little bodies playing, moving about, cuddling, hugging, jumping, and sleeping. Today was one of those busier days with a playdate at a friend's house followed by one at my own. During the typical hustle and bustle that comes with getting my boys in and out of the car, I was reminded of something. Peacefulness filled my heart as I observed the solace that comes to them as they rest in the knowledge that mommy is close by and won't ever leave them. It is something that my little Luke reminds me of whenever I tell him the agenda for the day. His response is always the question, "Mama right here?" I reassure him that I will be staying with him all day long, no matter where we go. After he hears my confident reply he smiles, laughs, and resumes his carefree activity. While playing, watching a movie, or sometimes even while eating, Luke will pose that same question: "Mama right here?" His face gleams with delight whenever I respond, "Yes, mama's right here." Lastly, "Mama right here?" is also asked at bedtime when it is time to stop reading and turn out the lights. "Mama's right here," I answer again, and he is overjoyed once more.

"Mama right here" reminds me that my little boy needs his mommy. He needs me to stay with him until he is asleep, and to accompany him while he learns to play and socialize with other children. This gives him the peace in his heart that mommy cares and loves him enough to be there no matter what. What a joy it is to be the best friend to my two beautiful baby boys. They both want and require their mommy alongside them in these fleeting, growing years. What consolation to be able to always respond, "Mama's right here."

Jesus, let me be a mother who is available and sensitive to the needs of my children so they will know I am always here for them.

Scripture of the Week:

Deuteronomy 31:6

Be strong and courageous. Do not be afraid or terrified because of them, for the LORD your God goes with you; he will never leave you nor forsake you.

Practical Weekly Application:

1. Spend time in *The Bible* and in prayer with God.
2. You may or may not be able to be there for every moment in the day to day with your child. However, this week make a list of occurrences in which your little one(s) truly needed their mommy and no one else. Praise God for the impact and the time you have to spend with your children and to be present in their lives!

"Mama Right Here"

5. Your Mommy

*N*ow that you are a mom, have you taken the time to thank your own mother for all she has done? When I had my first baby, I never dreamed of all the work it would entail to raise a child up until this point. My oldest is only two now, so I have a long way to go!

I wrote a short and simple poem for my mom's birthday this year instead of buying her a gift, and I think she cherishes this more than anything I could have bought. I have included what I wrote to her below:

Mommy

The word mommy conjures up so much, in just two syllables. It allows us to reminisce of younger years when life didn't have responsibilities and every day was filled with carefree moments with mommy always present to share them:

Root beer floats, walks around the block, visits to countless parks, hours of stories on mommy's lap, and stroller rides with mommy just for fun.

Ice cream truck treats, summer days filled with sprinklers, chalk drawing, and baby pool splashing with Barbies and mommy.

VBS with mommy as the craft queen, church picnics and celebrations with friends.

Family get-togethers at "our house," cousin sleepovers and midnight videos, and mommy's homemade breakfasts of French toast and pancakes.

Wintry days cozied up by the fire, mom preparing hot chocolate and all of us pitching in to frost cookies.

"Snow days" in which entire days were merrily spent outside building snowmen, forts, and snow angels. Mom faithfully bundling us up and then peeling off the wet layers of wintry dress after hours of delightful playtime.

So many memories, and just one name brought them all back: "mommy."

Love you mommy. Now I know in a much deeper way the weight and significance a mommy can be in a child's world. Thank you for instilling so much into me, and may God help me now to pass that on to my children.

Happy Birthday Mommy!
Love always,
Krystal Hope

∞ ∞ ∞

Jesus, thank you for my own earthly mother. Help me to show appreciation to her in the busyness of my days. May I extend and show forgiveness to her when needed, as I realize my own need for forgiveness.

Scripture of the Week:

Ephesians 6:1-3
Children, obey your parents in the Lord, for this is right. "Honor your father and mother"—which is the first commandment with a promise— "so that it may go well with you and that you may enjoy long life on the earth."

Practical Weekly Application:

1. Spend time in *The Bible* and in prayer with God.
2. If you have not said thank you to your mom recently, don't put it off. Write her a card, a poem, or a few short lines of gratitude for her life. If you have lost your mother, thank God for her and remember who she was. If your mom has really disappointed and/or hurt you, allow and pray for God's grace to flow over your heart towards her.
3. Reflect on the difficulties of motherhood in your own life and pray for God to allow you to move on and overcome any temptation to imitate past behavior that was hurtful.

Your Mommy

6. An Intentional Legacy

I wrote a little something about my youngest son, Bennett. Take a few minutes to write something to one or all of your children today. Put it in a safe place so that one day they can read it themselves, as it will be something they will treasure forever, and so will you.

Bennett:
You don't say much yet, but I know you will.
Your sweet and contented spirit makes my heart feel still.
Watching and waiting for the moment you smile, take your first step and begin to read
<u>*Lyle Lyle Crocodile.*</u>
So much to do, so little time,
Jesus, help me love my baby first, for he is now mine.
One day he will be "given away," though He was always Yours, to a sweet young girl,
who is serving the Lord.
Oh I can't comprehend it,
It is too much for now.
Oh help me to love him, to kiss him, to squeeze him,
For my dear "Benny Boo" is only here for a season.
I love you dearly, Bennett.

Here is an idea for you to try out this week: find a way to leave a trace of your thoughts for your child on a do-able basis. What has worked for me is to have notebooks for each of my boys in which I write them short letters every few months with updates on how they are growing, funny things they are doing or saying, and prayers for who they are becoming and how I see God working in them. Perhaps you would like to include drawings, photography, or music into memory boxes that your child can one day look back on and appreciate.

Scripture of the Week:

Psalm 127:3-5
Children are a heritage from the Lord, offspring a reward from him. Like arrows in the hands of a warrior are children born in one's youth. Blessed is the man whose quiver is full of them.

Practical Weekly Application:

1. Spend time in *The Bible* and in prayer with God.
2. Leave a trace of your thoughts for your child this week in some way. Also, see if you can find something small that will be maintainable to continue doing every once in a while for your child, to leave a special legacy of prayers, thoughts, and/or memories for your child to one day cherish.

An Intentional Legacy

7. The Word "Mommy"

I grew up saying this word many a time, but now that I am on the other end of it, it brings an entirely new sensation when it is spoken. "Mommy." I am now a mommy. How did this happen? Well, technically we all know that! But truly, how in such a short time did I transform from being a girl, woman, wife, pregnant woman, and now a mommy? When I ponder it, the thought seems a bit overwhelming, exhilarating, and unreservedly important all at once. "Mommy." So much in such a small utterance.

Yet, the mommy I long to be is one I know I cannot attain on my own. The moments when I feel anger, distress, and frustration after having to clean up spilled water on the kitchen floor for the umpteenth time just because my little boy wanted to experiment with dumping—those are the real testers of my "mommy hood." Am I worthy of being a mommy, with the constant responsibility and self-sacrifice that it requires? At times, I don't know. Yet, instead of wallowing in my failure and regrets, I choose to live another moment remembering the past victories and relishing in the present simple joys. I choose to tell my two-year-old son, "I'm sorry," and admit that mommy loses her temper at times and makes mistakes too. Maybe mommy should practice "time-out" on herself!

What blissful days we can CHOOSE to have when relying on our Savior Jesus for the peace and satisfaction that comes not from buying things, cleaning our house, or looking "put together". NO. The peace He offers ensures that my days are sprinkled with laughter, smiles, cooing, time-outs when needed, and love deeper than I could ever imagine.

"Mommy." It seems that this word encompasses something I may never fully be, yet desire to be. Help me, Lord, to keep on striving to be a godly, loving, patient, affectionate, compassionate, empathetic, fun, smart, and sensitive mommy to my children. I give you the glory for this, and pray that others would see my dependence on you for the "success."

Scripture of the Week:

Hebrews 4:14-16
Therefore, since we have a great high priest who has ascended into heaven, Jesus the Son of God, let us hold firmly to the faith we profess. For we do not have a high

priest who is unable to empathize with our weaknesses, but we have one who has been tempted in every way, just as we are—yet he did not sin. Let us then approach God's throne of grace with confidence, so that we may receive mercy and find grace to help us in our time of need.

Practical Weekly Application:

1. Spend time in *The Bible* and in prayer with God.
2. Make a list of the top three qualities you desire to exhibit to your children as their mommy. Pray and ask God to naturally develop these qualities into your being and personhood as a woman and as a mother.

The Word "Mommy"

8. I Choose to Laugh

*a*s a young mother, I love to revel in the small moments. The moments when my little baby is cooing at me, slobbering me with a wet kiss, reaching out his hands for mine, and giving mommy a hug "just because."

Yet, there are other moments that are mixed into my days—although I don't like to dwell on them. These moments sometimes include whining for no apparent reason, little tumbles and falls that result in tears and screams, and of course those good old-fashioned temper tantrums. I had one of those moments the other day.

My husband, Jorge, and I took our children to the mall for some family time. Luke fell asleep for his nap on the way, but his normal sleep time was cut in half when the car stopped. So, problem #1, Luke is tired. We decided to get some lunch at the mall, but the overcrowded food court meant Luke just didn't want to eat his hot dog. So, problem #2, Luke is hungry.

In my attempts to take Luke for a short walk after not having success feeding him, he escaped from my grip and wandered off towards the kid's play area with cars and other rides that cost a quarter or more to operate. I didn't have any money but he didn't realize it, as he is only two and was just as happy sitting in the toy vehicles. You may have guessed, that third problem came when I tried to convince Luke that it was time to go and leave his newfound toy wonderland. That's always a problem!

Well, Luke had a tantrum. On a scale of one to ten, ten being very loud and obnoxious, I would give it a seven. So, not too bad, considering! The point I want to make here is a choice we all have in moments like this, when our stress level rises as mothers, and we wish we could disappear. The option I took got me through those next "embarrassing moments" without losing it: I chose to laugh. Yes, and laugh I did! Luke still didn't think anything was funny, but that simple choice to laugh freed up my spirit that afternoon. It allowed me not only to survive the moment, but to love my child in spite of his ranting and raving. It felt so good to just laugh, and with that of course, came a smile to my face.

In moments where sin can so easily creep its way in and tempt to ensnare our hearts with poor attitudes and pent-up anger, choose to lighten up and give yourself permission to laugh. It may not stop what is about to happen, but it will instill within you a coping mechanism that I believe God created for our use.

Jesus, today I choose to laugh.

Scriptures of the Week:

Proverbs 29:17
Discipline your children, and they will give you peace; they will bring you the delights you desire.

Proverbs 17:22
A cheerful heart is good medicine, but a crushed spirit dries up the bones.

Practical Weekly Application:

1. Spend time in *The Bible* and in prayer with God.
2. Journal about some of the most stressful mothering moments you have had so far on your journey. Take time to laugh at the memories of crazy times past, and then make sure to add to your list this week as you continue experiencing them! Laugh!

I Choose to Laugh

9. The Importance of Mothering First

From the moment I wake up, the first thought in my mind now as a young mom is no longer what I would like to eat, when I would like to get up, or even what I would like to do that day. The majority of the time, my two little ones now dictate all of this. It is a strange phenomenon how quickly our world shifts from being so "me-focused" to "other-focused."

During year one of my first child's life, I remember almost a daily battle of surrender inside me. I had to learn how to lay down my own desires, comforts, and energies for the sake of my child.

When the world around us wants to fill our minds with notions of "me first," and "fulfill your own dreams no matter what the cost," we have to take a step back. As mothers, we now have a different calling that requires our full attention at all times. Apart from nurturing a strong relationship with your spouse, anything that comes between a mother and her relationship with her children is not what is best for her or for them. God desires a commitment from us to our children that is genuine, self-sacrificing, and real. Remember, He is the One who has entrusted us with the care of these precious miracles here on earth. Let us teach them to follow and serve Him. If we take this lightly, we are shirking our primary God-given role as mothers.

Jesus, help me to put my family at the forefront, and not the other way around.

Scripture of the Week:

Philippians 2:3-4
Do nothing out of selfish ambition or vain conceit. Rather, in humility value others above yourselves, not looking to your own interests but each of you to the interests of the others.

Practical Weekly Application:

1. Spend time in *The Bible* and in prayer with God.
2. Plan a special family time this week. If you are married, also plan a special date night just for the two of you. It doesn't have to be extravagant or expensive, but rather intentional and meaningful. If you can't get a sitter, plan a special evening at home after the kids' bedtime. Enjoy remembering that you, the mother, are a valued and faithful servant, first and foremost, to your family!

The Importance of Mothering First

10. A Peek into a Mother's Mind

*I*t is 6 a.m. on Monday. The next hour and a half is always a challenge, and yet the time seems to fly by. My boys are usually up between 6 and 7 a.m., which means it's time for morning snuggles, diaper changes, getting breakfast on the table and preparing my husband's lunchbox for work. In addition, I try to feed my own stomach while helping the kids chow down. By the time my husband walks down the stairs, dressed and ready to leave, everything is usually wrapping up. The kitchen that was sparkling clean the night before has once again exploded into a smorgasbord of dirty dishes, breakfast items and crumbs covering every inch of counter space!

Once daddy departs, the next item on the agenda is to clean up while managing to entertain my two young boys, ages two and nine months. The list goes on. Sound familiar?

Our days as mothers are often experienced moment to moment. Each moment, many small tasks are required of us as our children grow, such as feeding them, holding them, changing their dirty diapers, rocking them, reading to them, playing, loving on them, and so on. If we choose to see these moments as opportunities to nurture our little children, even in the smallest ways, I think we will find ourselves seizing each moment for what it is truly worth. Otherwise, we could end up getting so caught up in the "to do" list of each second that we miss finding the enjoyment we can offer to our babies.

So, sing your favorite song or play some kid's music while you clean up. Let your toddler or older child help you load the dishwasher. Don't just get through the moment, but live it to the fullest!

Jesus, help me to slow down today and even in the busyness of each moment give you glory.

Scripture of the Week:

Matthew 11:28-30
"Come to me, all you who are weary and burdened, and I will give you rest. Take my yoke upon you and learn from me, for I am gentle and humble in heart, and you will find rest for your souls. For my yoke is easy and my burden is light."

Practical Weekly Application:

1. Spend time in *The Bible* and in prayer with God.
2. Scratch the non-emergency items on the "to do" list this week and hunker down with your kids. Get on the floor and cuddle, read, tickle, and teach them. Journal about the simple memories that occurred without surrounding yourself with too many other "to-dos."

A Peek into a Mother's Mind

11. Much to Do, So Little Time

o you ever wake up tired? Okay, so I am not alone!

As moms, we know that on most days we would like to sleep in just a little longer. If you are like me, you slumber as long as you can. That is, until your "alarm clock" that exactly resembles a baby's cry goes off!

There is such sacrifice and denial of self in motherhood. I remember being extremely frightened of this brand-new journey I was on, as it seemed to never end. When my firstborn was only a few days old, I searched the internet for: "When will my child sleep through the night?!" It seems like the sleepless nights, the crying, and the constant diaper changes will never come to an end. Yet, time passes and those repetitive actions are vaguely remembered in comparison with the lasting gift that God has entrusted to you: your child.

Your child is God's creation, just as you are. Today, take hold of the thought that your mother made sacrifices while raising you, whether you had an adoptive or biological mom. Our earthly moms are not perfect, and neither are we. However, they too went through sleepless nights, countless temper tantrums, and may very well still suffer and hurt when we do.

If you woke up tired today, don't fret. These days are going to be more physically exhausting for a time, but try to tailor your routine around them. Do less and love more. Rock and kiss your baby, which may require fewer trips out to the store or a friend's house. Take time to nurture the simple relationship of mother and child today, and rest in the thought that God is using you to ultimately teach your little one of His love. Rest.

Jesus, the pressure to do more many times results in apparent efficiency without true quality. Fill me with your peace to do less and love more today.

Scripture of the Week:

Colossians 3:12-15

Therefore, as God's chosen people, holy and dearly loved, clothe yourselves with compassion, kindness, humility, gentleness and patience. Bear with each other and forgive one another if any of you has a grievance against someone. Forgive as the Lord forgave you. And over all these virtues put on love, which binds them all together in perfect unity. Let the peace of Christ rule in your hearts, since as members of one body you were called to peace. And be thankful.

Practical Weekly Application:

1. Spend time in *The Bible* and in prayer with God.
2. Plan a time of day where rest is central this week. If you are a working mom, make sure that you have time to put your feet up and unwind at home for even five or ten minutes before conquering other tasks. If you stay at home, build in some daily rest time so that you are refreshed to continue on each day to the best of your ability.

Much to Do, So Little Time

12. Emotionalism!

What struggles are you facing today as a young mom? I remember crying when my firstborn was only a week old, because I was pondering the thought of him going off to college already. After going through labor and experiencing a hard recovery, I felt like my body had just been literally broken. I was left in tears when I was told that I would have to pump for a time in addition to nursing. Struggles produce emotions. Strong emotions. We all have them.

As moms, we find it comforting to know that another mom has felt the same way as us. We have to stick together and not forget to share and be real with each other. Some of us are more emotional than others, but that doesn't mean we can't hear what they have gone through and relate in some way. What we have to do is make sure to put our emotions in check when they begin to govern and negatively affect our mood.

Typically, on the days when I am having a good day, my husband seems content and the house is peaceful. We all know the saying, "If mama ain't happy, ain't nobody happy." There is truth in these words, so they should create caution in us.

Mothers have been referred to as "the heart of the home" in many cultures around the world. We tend to be the ones that draw everyone together, even in extended family gatherings. Yet, we know that in our own flesh, our emotions could just as easily destroy us and leave a wake of destruction for those around. The only solution is to cry out to the living God for wisdom each day, beyond our momentary feelings, and to act against the current of our natural, human, sinful tendencies.

It's okay to be emotional at times, as life can be very trying and many situations will warrant strong emotions. On the other hand, let's not allow ourselves to be overly persuaded, bogged down, and carried by them, for Jesus invites us to cast our burdens on Him for He cares for us.

God, I am an emotional being. I want to reflect you in all aspects of my emotions. Take control of my emotions today.

Scripture of the Week:

1 Corinthians 6:19-20
Do you not know that your bodies are temples of the Holy Spirit, who is in you, whom you have received from God? You are not your own; you were bought at a price. Therefore, honor God with your bodies.

Practical Weekly Application:

1. Spend time in *The Bible* and in prayer with God.
2. Over the course of the week, make a list of some of the main emotions you feel throughout your days. They could be words like "stressed, calm, angry, or tired." Next to them write down any negative reactions you may have exhibited after feeling one of these emotions. Be in prayer to combat any emotional reactions and tendencies.

Emotionalism!

13. Hidden Treasures

At times I like to reflect on whether or not I've had a "good day" with my boys. Some days I "feel" good about the day simply because I know we had quality time together. Other days, it seems like the majority of the time was a struggle with whining, sickness, and sleep deprivation.

When my husband arrives home, he always asks how the day was. I usually give him a rundown of activities the boys and I did together, and try to get my two-year-old to articulate some of it to daddy. Yet, what about all the work I did that I didn't mention? All the boo-boo's that were kissed, the dirty diapers that were changed and now buried in a garbage, stroller rides to the park, chalk drawings washed away by rain, mounds of books read and stored away, and the goofy moments that resulted in giggles all around? So much of my work appears forgotten. It seems that all I have done for the day has vanished right before my eyes, and what is left at day's end is another dirty dinner table to tend to.

NO. The truth is there are hidden treasures that you are storing away today in your children's souls, into their very being. They know you are their caretaker, their best friend, and their mommy for all time.

So much can happen in our days as young moms. It is a wonderland of adventure if we can grasp hold of the diversity of teaching we can impart to our children while also learning ourselves. Put the cell phone away, don't check your email so much, and dive into life with your babies. There is a sweetness of togetherness in these short molding years. What is hidden now will become known one day. Store up hidden treasures, in your children.

Jesus, use my life as a beacon of light for my children to follow. Awaken your purposes in my day to day. Thank you, Lord.

Scripture of the Week:

Proverbs 22:6

Start children off on the way they should go, and even when they are old they will not turn from it.

Practical Weekly Application:

1. Spend time in *The Bible* and in prayer with God.
2. Make this week extra light in the "getting together with others" category. Allow your children to be nestled up in your lap, arms, and heart more than in any other place.

Hidden Treasures

14. Skeletons in Mommy's Closet?

$\mathcal{T}$he dreaded truth is that all of us as mothers have things that are buried away in our hearts and lives that we wouldn't dare share with others. These little "mommy secrets" may be big or small. I will share a few of my own.

I don't talk about this with many people, and still have a sense of dread in knowing that everyone who reads this book will know my "skeletons!" Nevertheless, as I was reflecting, I think my biggest skeleton right now has to do with what happens at night in our home. I have a two-year-old and a nine-month-old. I have not had a full night's sleep for months without at least one of them waking up. For a while it didn't bother me too much, but just yesterday I was feeling guilty about it. What am I doing wrong? I guess I don't beat myself up too much over my nine-month-old, as I know he is still growing and teething. But my two-year-old wakes up at least once per night to be reassured that mommy and daddy are here.

Another "night skeleton" is that either my husband or I have had to stay in the room with our oldest son on countless nights in order for him to fall asleep. I never thought I would be "that mom" with kids who can't go to bed on their own and who wake up at night crying even though I love on them all day. I am that mom. The mom with the imperfect kids, who is herself imperfect. Who am I? I think we struggle with these guilty mom feelings because we see our children as reflections of ourselves, and therefore we feel shame when they don't measure up to our standard of "perfection." In thinking along these lines, we fail to recall the humbling fact that this desire and expectation is rooted in selfishness and pride.

I know many moms out there have it much worse than I do, as I am sure the skeletons I shared are nothing compared to what other mothers are facing. Yet, no matter what your skeletons are, I believe God wants to obliterate the anxiety and fear that Satan tries to implant in you when facing them.

I also believe that you should share these skeletons and struggles with some of your trustworthy, safe friends who are also mothers. Motherhood is a journey, and you need company along the way. If you can't be real with others, how will they ever go deeper with you? Be the one to open up a discussion that allows for healing in some of the "off limit" areas of motherhood.

Jesus, use me today to share some vulnerable territory that I have traversed or am currently traversing in motherhood with trustworthy friends. Allow me to listen and not judge when others share these areas with me as well.

Scripture of the Week:

Ephesians 4:25
Therefore each of you must put off falsehood and speak truthfully to your neighbor, for we are all members of one body.

Practical Weekly Application:

1. Spend time in *The Bible* and in prayer with God.
2. Contact one friend that you trust, preferably someone who is a mother as well. Share a vulnerable area of motherhood with her (one of your "skeletons"). She will probably share one too, without you even asking!

Skeletons in Mommy's Closet?

15. Impossible Means NOT Possible!

W aking up and thinking about how to accomplish my endless "to do" list may bring about exhaustion and defeat before the day even begins. The perfect garden, always clean kitchen, emptied laundry baskets, and vacuumed house are duties in our day but shouldn't be our first priorities. I am reminded of this reality every time I have a lot to do in the morning in order to get somewhere. Let me share one such scenario that played itself out a few days ago.

When the morning began, I already knew I had to be ready a bit earlier, as a mommy friend of mine and her little girl were on their way over for an outside playdate. I decided to make banana bread, as we had run out of store-bought bread that morning. That decision cost me the peace that I desperately wanted!

I tried to whip up the banana bread with my toddler and nine-month-old circling around me in the kitchen. The voice in my head kept saying, "Slow down, read with them." I thought I needed the bread to eat and feed to my family. All I remember now are the whines, moans, and mini temper-tantrums that my toddler was pulling to try and get my attention. Finally, I took both my boys, popped them in the double stroller, and went on a short jog just before my friend arrived. This was my attempt to clear the heavy air of stress and frustration that was lurking in our home, or perhaps just in my head!

Sometimes our view of ourselves is so wrapped up in how successful our day is. We feel worthless or unproductive if everything we were hoping for was not accomplished. Here is where we need a gentle yet firm reminder as mothers: We cannot do it all, for that is impossible and impossible means NOT possible.

As much as I like to think of myself as "superwoman," in the depths of my heart I know it is all just a facade. I cannot tend the garden, read books to my boys, clean every dish, change every diaper, look put-together, and have all the laundry folded and stored away every day. Impossible. NOT possible. Remind yourself of this when you start to feel overwhelmed. I have the tendency to want to prove I am in charge via the appearance of my home and the behavior of my children. In an effort to control our days, we can easily create an unattainable standard for ourselves that centers around productivity. The quicker we learn this lesson the less guilt, control, and ugliness we will endure.

Jesus, thank you that my value as a mother is not in what I do but in who YOU are. As I press into you each day, remind me that no matter what I accomplish today, if I can glorify you in all of it I have done my best.

Scripture of the Week:

Ecclesiastes 3:9-14
What do workers gain from their toil? I have seen the burden God has laid on the human race. He has made everything beautiful in its time. He has also set eternity in the human heart; yet no one can fathom what God has done from beginning to end. I know that there is nothing better for people than to be happy and to do good while they live. That each of them may eat and drink, and find satisfaction in all their toil—this is the gift of God. I know that everything God does will endure forever; nothing can be added to it and nothing taken from it. God does it so that people will fear him.

Practical Weekly Application:

1. Spend time in *The Bible* and in prayer with God.
2. Be comfortable this week with accomplishing much less. Have two do-able goals in mind for each day, such as complete two loads of laundry and have dinner started by 4:30 p.m. Anything else that you may get to in a given day will be a celebration of extreme accomplishment (not a mundane, expected, and predictable achievement).

Impossible Means NOT Possible!

16. Mommy Doubles

*N*o one can ever replace the role God has given you as the mother of your children. Yet, I have found great refuge in knowing that I have found a few "mommy doubles," as I have termed them. These women can accompany me almost anywhere and be there with me to care for my precious babies. Grandmothers are obvious choices for this special role! In my life, two of these mommy doubles are my sisters, and one is a close and dear friend. These women are indispensable because many times the key to enjoyment at a park, zoo, or mall is just knowing you are not alone.

Especially now that I have two little boys, I appreciate and recognize the need to have helpers in order to have a successful, safe, and pleasurable trip to most places outside my home! Trying to always conquer tasks with our children on our own isn't always a bad thing, but many times the stress of it all can remove the fun and relaxation that we seek to gain and provide to our children. Hence, seek some "mommy doubles" for your next outing.

Jesus, help me to lay down my pride and admit I can't do it all. Provide close friends and family to come alongside me to nurture and lend a helping hand to me while my babies are growing and learning. Thank you, Lord.

Scripture of the Week:

Ecclesiastes 4:9-12
Two are better than one, because they have a good return for their labor: If either of them falls down, one can help the other up. But pity anyone who falls and has no one to help them up.

Practical Weekly Application:

1. Spend time in *The Bible* and in prayer with God.

2. Plan an outing this week and invite a "mommy double" to come along. Let this "mommy double" know in advance that you will need some assistance and that you thought of him or her specifically for this task. If you can't think of someone, ask God to open your eyes to who this could be and/or to place someone in your life that you can trust in this way.

Mommy Doubles

17. Mommy is My Princess

I remember as a little girl looking up to my mommy in so many ways. As I grew, I remember looking at her and wishing I had more of her features: her green eyes, kissable lips, and even her lower height. (I am a few inches taller!)

Whether you have little baby girls or little baby boys, both will grow to adore you, their mommy. Do you ever contemplate how neat this is? You are like a princess or hero to your children in many ways. You are the one they've learned to go to for every need since they were born, and the one they look to for advice and comfort when they're down. None of us deserve to have such admiration, but there is One who does.

In the midst of your day, do you refresh yourself with prayer, reading God's word, and quiet times of being still before the Lord? I speak to myself very much when I write this, as I know as a mom there are a million and one excuses to NOT stop and sit quietly.

God has given us little gifts wrapped up in tiny bodies to love, care for and teach. Teach them through your example that mommy depends on Jesus for all her "strength" and that her beauty inside and out comes from Our Heavenly Father.

Jesus, allow me to radiate you so that my children will one day realize it is YOU in me.

Scripture of the Week:

Isaiah 54:13
All your children will be taught by the LORD, and great will be their peace.

Practical Weekly Application:

1. Spend time in *The Bible* and in prayer with God.

2. Make spending time with God a priority this week. Make it a point to journal scriptures that you come across and work on memorizing at least one of them.

Mommy is My Princess

18. Noise

To say there is "a lot of noise" in my house right now seems like an understatement! I have a toddler and a nine-month-old who thinks he is already a one-year-old! These two little men, whom I love dearly, have captured my heart and my ears! Babbling, whining, singing, giggling, screaming, cooing, and boo-hooing. There aren't a lot of quiet moments anymore, which can lead me to feel ever grateful for even a few spare minutes of silence!

How often do we let the noise in our days deafen us to God's still, small voice in our lives? No matter when or how, we all need at least a few quiet moments every day to spend with the Lord and refresh our souls for His use. We truly have nothing to offer if we aren't being filled up in God's presence. God's Word is a tool that we have access to in which HE can speak directly to us, and can mold us as young mothers into women that seek after His Kingdom above all else.

I myself struggle with leaving my children at times, even for a short period, as I desire to give them my undivided attention and love as much as possible. I need to remind myself that if I never take a break and get alone with God, I will soon resent my duties and become apathetic towards God's leading and unaware of my own emptiness without His work in my heart.

Even if it is only five minutes, take the time to tame the noise in your life by spending your quiet time with Jesus today.

Scripture of the Week:

1 Chronicles 16:8-11
Give praise to the LORD, proclaim his name; make known among the nations what he has done. Sing to him, sing praise to him; tell of all his wonderful acts. Glory in his holy name; let the hearts of those who seek the LORD rejoice. Look to the LORD and his strength; seek his face always.

Practical Weekly Application:

1. Spend time in *The Bible* and in prayer with God.
2. Take time this week to get away from the hustle and bustle of noise in your life. When the kids are in bed or napping, take the first five to ten minutes of that quiet time to go before the Lord. Pray to Him, read His Word, or perhaps listen to or sing a worship song that exalts His name.

Noise

19. Mommy Time

I know I like to write about all the joys of mothering and being there alongside your children as much as possible. Yet, we still need to consider the notion of personal refreshment apart from your children. If your constant attention and focus are consumed only with your family and their well-being, you will find that eventually you will be drained and unable to serve them as you desire to.

A solution to this is identifying something that could bring life and renewal to yourself, so you can thrive in your roles as a mom and a wife. Make a list of things that you enjoy, and then find some time each day, or at least a few times a week, to dabble in them.

My boys currently take afternoon naps, so that is my best opportunity to refresh myself. There are days when I mow the lawn or work in the garden while they rest, and other days when I sit down to write. It seems that all can be "amiss," but if I have had even ten minutes of time to myself, there seems to be order where otherwise I would feel chaos and havoc.

If today is a day where the kids are sick and things are not going as planned, be creative in how you find a little time for yourself. Maybe this means the kids can play quietly or watch a video for a bit while you sip a chai latte!

Jesus, thank you for equipping me to be a godly mother to my children each day. Fill me up in my quiet time with you and provide an outlet of personal creativity so that I can express the talents you have given me.

Scripture of the Week:

Psalm 23:1-2
The Lord is my shepherd, I lack nothing. He makes me lie down in green pastures, he leads me beside quiet waters.

Practical Weekly Application:

1. Spend time in *The Bible* and in prayer with God.
2. Make a list of three things you would like to do in your "spare time." The list should be comprised of enjoyable pastimes for you. After making the list, make sure to write down how you will accomplish these things by carving out time in your day to do so. Perhaps an idea could be going out with a friend(s) to catch up and relax, so plan ahead for childcare and enjoy your night out mama!

Mommy Time

20. Happy with a Toilet Cap

The other day my nine-month-old son, Bennett, scurried with all the energy he could muster into our downstairs bathroom. I entered to find him smiling from ear to ear with one simple object: a white toilet bolt cap in his hand! Happy with a toilet cap!

As we go through our days, what drives us as mothers? Do we seek happiness from the praise of others for "perfect days" where our imperfect children never have a bad moment? If we are waiting for days like that, they will never come.

Last week I remember looking forward to naptime, as I usually do, for the simple pleasure of having some time to myself. Instead of taking a nap, one of my boys simply wanted to play. I decided that I would hold him for a while and see what he would do in my arms. Those next few moments were unforgettable, as I have never seen him so focused on my face and expressions! He wanted to be cradled in my arms and look and laugh at mommy! The giggles and tender affection from that time together was worth the nap he skipped in the moment. Yet, how many times have I gotten upset that my little one wouldn't fall asleep right when I desired him to? How many cuddles have I missed because I am so focused on fulfilling a routine?

Many times we miss the opportunity to bond in simple ways with our babies because we, as adults, have a laundry list of to-dos each day that we want to check off before we can enjoy our children. We are all guilty of this, because we have been brought up in a society where work is praised and vacation time is something you do a few weeks out of the year, if you're lucky. Remember, you are a MOTHER. This includes maintaining a functional home in the practical sense of dishes and laundry, but those tasks should never take precedence over all the small moments of tender love between mother and child.

Children are such a picture of God's heart. Let us learn from them and be happy with the "toilet cap."

Jesus, I want to be a mom that is present for my children. Teach me how to balance my to-do list and my children's needs.

Scripture of the Week:

Philippians 4:11-12

I am not saying this because I am in need, for I have learned to be content whatever the circumstances. I know what it is to be in need, and I know what it is to have plenty. I have learned the secret of being content in any and every situation, whether well fed or hungry, whether living in plenty or in want.

Practical Weekly Application:

1. Spend time in *The Bible* and in prayer with God.
2. Ask God to instill in your heart this week a sense of gratitude that is supernatural. Despite the day-to-day grind, ask God to awaken a joy and an energetic spirit that seeks to live each moment to the fullest for His glory!

Happy with a Toilet Cap

21. All Too Fast

*I*t seems tragic to speak of a time when our little babies will no longer be little anymore. Okay, I am sure there are days when you, like me, wish they were bigger and more capable of doing tasks a bit more independently! However, the loss of having babies or young children can seem depressing as we know every baby will eventually, one day, become a young child, an adolescent, and even an adult!

Although I cannot speak to you yet as a mother who has lived through and been a part of each of these precious stages, I am a daughter who has gone through them myself. Looking back, I remember the times when I thought my mom knew it all and was the loveliest mommy and person in the whole world. I recollect how my mom slowly switched over from being an authority in my life to more of a friend in recent years. In the past I appreciated her for what I knew then. But now with the passage of time and having my own little ones, I can rightly feel gratitude for the depth of her motherhood in our lives as children, and even up until now. A mother never ceases being a mother!

My mother was able to stay at home with us during the day, producing many fond memories of times together. We were also privileged to have my dad's workplace close enough to our home that he could eat all his meals with us. I remember those days, as I am no longer present at my parents' dinner table every day. Yet, I am reliving such traditions of family time in the home God has given to me, with my own children and husband.

A widow at a mom's group I attended spoke to this, as she shared how she still longs for the days when her husband was alive and present in her home. The picture is ever-changing; all too fast a new season will be upon us. Grasp hold of the season you are in, love it for all it is worth, and pray through the challenges it presents. Remember, it is just a season passing by.

Jesus, thank you for the unique seasons we go through in our lives. Despite the difficulties that I am facing today in this season, give me eyes to see Your mighty hand over it all.

Scripture of the Week:

Ecclesiastes 3:1-8

There is a time for everything, and a season for every activity under the heavens: a time to be born and a time to die, a time to plant and a time to uproot, a time to kill and a time to heal, a time to tear down and a time to build, a time to weep and a time to laugh, a time to mourn and a time to dance, a time to scatter stones and a time to gather them, a time to embrace and a time to refrain from embracing, a time to search and a time to give up, a time to keep and a time to throw away, a time to tear and a time to mend, a time to be silent and a time to speak, a time to love and a time to hate, a time for war and a time for peace.

Practical Weekly Application:

1. Spend time in *The Bible* and in prayer with God.
2. Journal about the season of life you are in, including the highs and the lows. Cry out to Him for wisdom and strength to face the challenges and heartaches, and yet shout praise to His name for the unique blessings you are receiving now that will someday be but a fond memory.

All Too Fast

22. Grateful

*T*oday was a day of reflection for me. It was a crisp fall morning, and I watched as children walked to their bus for the first day of school. I felt a surpassing sense of relief that my two little lambs were still with me, and I held them closer and kissed them more just pondering it. Perhaps because only a year prior I was still working as a teacher, longing for the day when I could fulfill the desire God placed in my heart to be a stay-at-home mom. I remembered the tears that were shed on a daily basis when I had to say goodbye to my firstborn, Luke, and head off to work until God provided my husband with a job.

So, on that morning I decided to take my boys to the playground by the elementary school that they will attend if we send them to public school, which is the same school that I attended as a child. As I went down the tall slide with my two pumpkins nestled on my lap, life seemed wonderfully peaceful and glorious. I posed the question in my mind: How did I get so lucky? How do I get to spend every day with my little men? Despite the good times and the bad, they are my gifts from the Lord and I treasure this experience. I know it will be all too soon before I will be that mom sending her little boy off to school, wondering what happened to the time, and how my days will be altered with one "missing" from the nest. Once again the realization hit me of how incredibly blessed I am to be a mom to my two babies, and to share these unforgettable years together.

Let us take time to ponder the many wonders of Our God. They come in the forms of little bodies moving about, as well as in the numerous ways He provides and sustains us each day. If we don't have grateful hearts as women, as mothers, we won't be able to help our children cultivate this important trait.

Financially tight budgets? Crying babies? Sleepless nights? Endless laundry? We are so blessed. Be grateful in the face of adversity. How is this possible? Not with our own strength, so lean on HIM.

Jesus, give me Your vision and heart of gratitude. Let me not dwell on what lacks, but rather on what I am lacking: gratefulness. I am so grateful for all you have done for me this past year. I love you.

Scripture of the Week:

1 Thessalonians 5:18
Give thanks in all circumstances; for this is God's will for you in Christ Jesus.

Practical Weekly Application:

1. Spend time in *The Bible* and in prayer with God.
2. Make a list of ten things you can think of that you are grateful for today. If you have people on your list, be sure to let them know of your appreciation for their influence in your life by way of a phone call, card, or even a visit.

Grateful

23. Cheap Fun

*A*t this point in life with my two boys, we don't have a lot of extra money lying around. My husband and I both agreed that I would stay at home with our children during these growing years. Although it can be seen as a financial sacrifice, I have found creative ways to have fun without dishing out any cash. Here are a few ideas for family entertainment without breaking the bank:

- ***Buy a local zoo or museum membership*** that you think your family/children will all enjoy. Invest in the admission and use it on a rainy day when you are looking for something free and fun to do together!
- ***Take a relaxing car ride*** during the morning, afternoon, or evening together as a family. Bring along a book you could read, a sermon to listen to, or be intentional with your conversations. For part of the ride, pick a few favorite worship songs to play and reflect together on Gods' goodness as you look out your windows. Price: FREE (besides a few dollars for gas!)
- ***Family movie night in pajamas!*** Pick a wholesome movie you know everyone will enjoy and benefit from watching. Break out the popcorn, drinks, and snacks! Let everyone bring a blanket and cozy up together. Price: FREE if you have a movie and a few snacks from your pantry.
- ***Craft day.*** Gather together any art supplies that you have lying around your house. Think of a theme based on the current season or time of year. For example, if it is fall you may want to do a craft involving leaves. If your kids are very young, come up with a simple project they can do with minimal help from you. If your kids are older, allow them a bit of creative liberty and guide them in discussing a craft idea that is do-able with their artistic input and current abilities. It can be as simple as drawing the first letter or letters of the current season on a piece of paper and decorating them with stickers, leaves, cotton balls, etc. Price: FREE
- ***Cooking time.*** Pick out a fun recipe for cookies, cake, or whatever your heart desires, and make it a family affair to prepare that dessert or dish together! Give each child a different job so that all feel useful and involved. Afterwards,

you could make enjoying your treat even more special by playing music, lighting candles, and dancing in the living room! All you will need are helping hands and some ingredients. Price: the cost of ingredients, many of which you may have already have in your pantry.

- ***Out to the park.*** Wait for a nicer day, and if you have any parks near you, go to one that you and your kids will enjoy playing at together. If you want to be a bit more active, take them to a park with a tennis court, soccer field, or basketball court, and have some fun "playing sports" together! While the kids are running, even if they aren't really learning the sport per se, you can kick or hit the ball around and get out some energy! Price: FREE

These ideas may seem simple and unimpressive, and they should! That is because they require a heart that longs for deep fellowship more than an impressive and over the top activity. If we can teach our children that being together trumps the circumstances or agenda, we have taught them well.

Jesus, give me a simple mind to once again dive into being a caring and carefree mommy for my husband and my children. Allow me to see that in the mundane there can be great rewards if I choose to see with Your eyes and seize each moment for Your glory.

Scripture of the Week:

Philippians 4:19
And my God will meet all your needs according to the riches of his glory in Christ Jesus.

Practical Weekly Application:

1. Spend time in *The Bible* and in prayer with God.
2. Choose at least one activity this week from my list, or from your own list of creative ways to have cheap fun, and do it together as a family! Perhaps it will turn into a weekly or monthly habit that will help your budget and ensure quality family and/or couple time together.

Cheap Fun

24. Try a New Routine

ays, weeks, months and years go by. They say it takes thirty days to develop a habit and only one day to break it. I have definitely found this to be true!

As moms we try to be somewhat consistent with routine to provide a sense of order and establish organization for ourselves and our children. Maybe you have a routine for bedtime that works for you. At times I have stuck to my routine for the sake of sticking to my routine, and yet have become frustrated in the midst of it. Why? I have realized that not every routine that I have established works or should be continued, and that at times I only stick to it in an attempt to feel good about myself.

For example, I had the routine of putting my boys in bed every day around 1:00 p.m. for naps. During one particularly challenging season, my older son Luke was refusing a nap at that specific time. Instead of embracing a bit of flexibility in our established routine and waiting until he was more ready for a rest, I would frustrate myself trying to put an untired toddler to sleep no matter how long it took. Reading your child's signals of hunger, exhaustion, and comfort are important in knowing when to intervene and when to wait.

At this point, I have one little boy who goes to bed between 8:00 and 8:30 p.m., and another who usually isn't tired until 9:00 or 9:30 p.m. Both still take their afternoon naps together, but one needs to stay up a little longer before he really needs to conk out for the night. Can I handle two different bedtimes for right now? YES. Will I eventually be able to have one bedtime for both boys? Probably. Hopefully! What is the key here? PATIENCE!

Sometimes our desires or goals as moms become expectations that we feel our children need to fulfill every day OR ELSE. Or else what? Or else we somehow are failures as moms because our children go to bed thirty minutes later? The attitude of a mother's heart should never be to "fulfill" a bedtime routine for the sake of getting it over with and feeling in control. Although it is wise and necessary for us to establish routines and structure to create order and security in our home, that should never trump God's love for our children and their best interests. Sometimes it is in their best interest to cuddle for a few more minutes with mommy or daddy on the couch, or read another book or two, instead of squeezing out a "routine."

Jesus, allow me to be filled with Your love towards my children to such an extent that I no longer desire to serve an idol of "routines," but rather cry out for more of YOU in my weakness. Help me to be a mommy that provides a healthy yet balanced structure for my children.

Scripture of the Week:

Romans 12:2
Do not conform to the pattern of this world, but be transformed by the renewing of your mind. Then you will be able to test and approve what God's will is—his good, pleasing and perfect will.

Practical Weekly Application:

1. Spend time in *The Bible* and in prayer with God.
2. Break your routine this week, in some way. If this is very scary for you, pray for peace and freedom in this area. You may try reading to your child/children for ten more minutes before bedtime, being a sillier mama and playing dress-up during the day with "old" clothes, or taking an afternoon nap instead of cleaning while your baby is sleeping! Whatever you decide to change, make sure you change it!

Try a New Routine

25. What to Tell a New Mom?

*I*f you are a new mom yourself, read these words with pause! If you are a little farther down the course, you will be able to smile.

Dear new mom,

First of all, welcome aboard the mommy train! You have now joined the ranks of women who have the privilege of caring for a little life for the rest of their lives.

I don't want to be pessimistic, but rather realistic with you. That is why I must tell you that this journey will start off very rocky, and each mother has her own unique and all-encompassing challenges that will arise with mothering a newborn or young baby.

You may have heard or be well aware of the sleep deprivation that comes with the territory, but until you yourself go through it, it pales in comparison to what you expect. The 24/7 around-the-clock care and attention with endless diapers to change, baths to give, and feeding sessions can seem very fatiguing. Days will seem long and endless, as your new normal will be watching the clock to calculate when your little one may be hungry again or just need you.

Yet, if you persevere long enough, suddenly a change will take place. In the midst of your foggy, tired state of mind, you will begin to adjust to the tiny miracle God has given to you. Never forget where this little one came from, and how he/she longs to be in YOUR arms above anywhere else.

The bad news is that being responsible for a new life takes a lot of energy, time, and devotion. The really bad news is you are never going to feel qualified for the task or one hundred percent ready. But hold on, because the great news is that you are not supposed to do it alone, which is probably why God made it so challenging to begin with.

Being a young mother will remind us of our inadequacies and OUR need for dependence. Yet, don't stay there, because there is more good news! God does His

73

greatest work, bringing hope in times like these. All we have to do is throw our hands up in the air and admit we can't, but He can. He did. Jesus took our place on the cross and died for all so that we can be assured of our eternity with God through accepting Jesus's sacrifice as the forgiveness of our sins as well as to give us new life here.

What can this new life look like as a mom? It looks like crying out to God in honesty, admitting you must have Him be the One who ultimately takes care of your little one(s) and you as well. It is not a ritualistic prayer, but rather a humble cry that must spring forth on a daily basis.

Jesus, You alone gave me the privilege of being a mother. I admit I can't do this on my own and don't want to, either. Take control of my life today, and release your strength into my aching and tired body. Thank you for this miracle of life, which is so tiny and precious at this moment, but with which you desire to do great and mighty things! Amen.

Scripture of the Week:

Isaiah 40:28-31
Do you not know? Have you not heard? The LORD is the everlasting God, the Creator of the ends of the earth. He will not grow tired or weary, and his understanding no one can fathom. He gives strength to the weary and increases the power of the weak. Even youths grow tired and weary, and young men stumble and fall; but those who hope in the LORD will renew their strength. They will soar on wings like eagles; they will run and not grow weary, they will walk and not be faint.

Practical Weekly Application:

1. Spend time in *The Bible* and in prayer with God.
2. Cry out to God this week and admit you are incapable of being a loving and godly mom on your own. Focus on the cross and on how through Christ alone you can have access to a God who makes us all new, if we surrender our lives to Him.

What to Tell a New Mom?

26. Formula for our Days?

lean the bathroom: check. Empty the garbage: check. Change a diaper: check. Change another diaper (probably a poopy one this time): check. Find little one in bathroom making a mess and clean bathroom yet again: check!

Sound familiar? It is natural as human beings to want to be productive, which is a good thing. Today efficiency is highly regarded as a professional skill, which usually involves multitasking. These skill sets become second nature to so many of us moms, yet perhaps to our downfall on occasion. Sometimes the desire to accomplish a task, which in and of itself is not wrong, can overtake my heart and mind and dictate the success or failure I feel as a mother. That is incorrect.

If I get ninety percent of the laundry washed and folded on Monday, but on Thursday can't seem to do any of it, did I fail? No. What you might fail to consider in that way of thinking is that your own pride and sense of self-worth is no longer from the Lord, but rather attached to the achievement of your own accomplishments.

The assumption here lies in a belief that there is a special "formula for our days" that we must conquer. Laundry done, dishes washed and dried, house in order, kids somewhat clean and dressed, and me at least with my teeth brushed! What if the formula doesn't work every day? What if I spend a little more time reading the Bible and don't quite finish dinner on time, or can't conquer washing, folding, and putting away every bit of laundry on a given day? What will happen? Nothing. At least as long as you don't let yourself feel ashamed and guilty for it. Communicate to your husband that each day has its own challenges and demands. He needs to know that although a clean and tidy house is wonderful, there will be many days in which that goal won't be achieved until he is home to help you! Marriage in general is teamwork, and raising a family is no exception. On those harder days, kindly remind your husband you need help, and don't let the guilt of failure overtake you no matter what his initial reaction may be. Your kids will still love you (even if they have to wait one more day to wear their favorite shirts), and God will still call you His if you are following Him first and foremost.

Jesus, may the formula for my day be YOUR purposes before my own. If nothing else is done today, may YOU at least be glorified in how I act and react to those around me. Praise Your name!

Scripture of the Week:

Colossians 3:23
Whatever you do, work at it with all your heart, as working for the Lord, not for human masters.

Practical Weekly Application:

1. Spend time in *The Bible* and in prayer with God.
2. This week write down what you were able to accomplish at the end of each day. This is an exercise not in discouragement, but rather a reality check so that you no longer think every day will yield the same results!

Formula for our Days?

27. Unforgettable Moments

There are moments that you will want to cherish and cling to as moms; moments when your child behaves perfectly at a playdate, says "thank you" without being prodded, gives you a hug just because, and dozes off in your arms with the most heavenly countenance.

Right now my two little ones are napping, and I just had one of those moments as I was putting my two-year-old to bed. Sometimes we cuddle together before he falls asleep, and that is what we did today. I was lying next to him reminding him it was time for him to close his eyes and stop talking. He was so happy that I was by his side. His smile beamed from ear to ear and he started to giggle from time to time while trying to settle in. Right before we both fell asleep I started to feel something on my face: kisses from my little boy with a smacking sound he had recently started practicing, so they would sound just like mommy's! Not only did I receive sweet, gentle kisses, but afterwards those sacred words mommies everywhere long to here: "I love you." My heart was alive! My almost two-and-a-half-year-old is finally expressing his love for me without any coaxing on my part, to my utmost delight! What joyfulness filled my heart as we both fell fast asleep next to each other after such a relished moment.

Several weeks have passed since, and now my little boy tells me "I love you" fairly often. Yet, I want to be determined not to let those words mean less and less the more they are spoken, because the meaning behind them is still the same. My little boy wants me to know he loves me, his mommy. If I fail to convey my love for him as faithfully, how will he ever understand the depths of God's love for him?

The beauty in all of this is what the Bible says about children. It states in Mark 10:14-15, "Let the little children come to me, and do not hinder them, for the kingdom of God belongs to such as these. I tell you the truth, anyone who will not receive the kingdom of God like a little child will never enter it".

How much can I learn from my two-year-old who easily forgives me when I lose my temper? Am I able to offer correction with love and forgiveness to him after he has a tantrum? We can learn from our little children.

Jesus, help me to be a beacon of your light and love to my children. Fill me with your surpassing love that knows no bounds, that I too may exemplify Your faithful devotion for my children to watch.

Scripture of the Week:

Matthew 19:13-14
Then people brought little children to Jesus for him to place his hands on them and pray for them. But the disciples rebuked them. Jesus said, "Let the little children come to me, and do not hinder them, for the kingdom of heaven belongs to such as these."

Practical Weekly Application:

1. Spend time in *The Bible* and in prayer with God.
2. Be intentional this week about looking for unforgettable moments, as small as they may seem, throughout your day. Jot them down before you forget them and then take time to ask Jesus to help you see these moments more and more, despite other more difficult moments and trials that may arise.

Unforgettable Moments

28. My Little Boy is Growing Up... Into What?

*L*uke has been really into superheroes for the past few months, and now is also showing quite an interest in the *Toy Story* movies and characters. His favorite seemed to be Buzz Light-year for a while, then Woody and Bullseye, and then.... oh my. You're not going to believe it but my little man was a little over two-and-a-half when he started blushing one day after he saw Jessie's picture in a *Toy Story* book! Now every time Jessie is mentioned he has a sheepish look as he says she is pretty and buries part of his face in his elbow! My little boy is growing up, already.

We can get so caught up at this stage in the little "gotta dos" of diaper changes, potty training, disciplining, feeding, and playing, that we can't fully wrap our heads around the idea that these little bodies will soon grow into adults. Reflect this week on your little one now, and then envision them in ten, fifteen, or even twenty years. It's not easy, I know, but ask God to help you and think on this for a short time. What do you long to see as traits and characteristics in your adult child? What times will you miss and always treasure when his or her body is no longer pint-size anymore for you to rock and hold? Let this experience cast vision into your day-to-day this week of how motherhood holds such worth even in the "gotta dos" of each day.

Jesus, my little one is growing up right before my eyes whether I see it now or not. There is so much purpose and pleasure that can be captured if I choose to see the masterpiece that you desire to make of my child. Thank you for allowing me to have a part in molding my children into Your image.

Scripture of the Week:

Genesis 1:27

So God created mankind in his own image, in the image of God he created them; male and female he created them.

Practical Weekly Application:

1. Spend time in *The Bible* and in prayer with God.
2. Do the reflection exercise listed in the second to last paragraph. Write down your responses and vision for your child here in the journal page.

My Little Boy is Growing Up...Into What?

29. Mommy Marker Discoveries

I have coined "mommy markers" as being anything and everything that tell you at this stage in your life, "I am a mother of young children." Here are the true "mommy markers" in my world as of now. You may have some of the same ones and others too.

Mashed bananas at the bottom of my purse, a forgotten poopy diaper found in the diaper bag or a random room in the house, a mascara "mask" created by my two-year-old all over his face, cookie crumbs adorning the car's seats and floor mats at all times, late nights rocking a teething baby, wet hands from toilet bowl "experimentation," toys in every corner imaginable, sticky hands, muddy faces, dishes always patiently waiting to be washed, cries every so often, smiles galore, and much more.

I could go on, but why? You all fully understand that motherhood entails an endless list of to-dos and only a few things we can say "done" to every day. Yet, these mommy markers are precious memories in and of themselves. Make a list of some "mommy markers" you have experienced within the past week. Take a moment to laugh at them. When you experience more of these in the future, call them your blessed "motherly markers" and laugh out loud even if you really want to cry!! (Remember, laughter is the best medicine, isn't it?!)

Without fruit in our lives, can we say we are Christians? The true mark of a Christian, as Paul says in 1 Corinthians, is the fruit of the spirit. He also reminds us in James 2:17 that "faith without works is dead." Just as we see "mommy markers" that remind us of our current stage of motherhood, so we need to be awakened to the "fruit" in our own Christian walk. What are the fruits of the spirit? Love, joy, patience, peace, kindness, goodness, faithfulness, gentleness and self-control (Galatians 5:22-23). Maybe your friends see some of these in your life, but does Jesus see them? That means, what are you like at your worst? We can all improve, and the closer we become to Jesus, the more fruit we will naturally bear. That is the simple truth, so stop making excuses and prioritize your day around Him first dear one.

Jesus, the true mark of a mother is YOU. Let me press in to you and Your words today, that I might be awakened to how much more of a mark You desire to make on me. I need YOU to do this work, yet help me be faithful with my part, surrendering my time and energy in order to be used by You.

Scripture of the Week:

Galatians 5:22-23
But the fruit of the Spirit is love, joy, peace, forbearance, kindness, goodness, faithfulness, gentleness and self-control. Against such things there is no law.

Practical Weekly Application:

1. Spend time in *The Bible* and in prayer with God.
2. Make a list of the "mommy markers" in your life, as described above. Then, make a list of some of the "fruit" you have seen in your Christian walk recently. Pray that more fruits would be developed and evident in your life!

Mommy Marker Discoveries

30. Angry Mama

While on vacation, I had a confrontation with my anger. We were visiting relatives in New Jersey, and my little man had helped me scrape out all the seeds from three butternut acorn squashes. After they were cooked, he was insisting on helping scoop out the soft and mushy squash with a "grown-up" spoon alongside mommy. I was feeling quite proud of my little boy, and glad that I could amuse him while we were preparing dinner. The trouble came when I took out the black pepper and set it on the counter. I turned my back for an instant to grab butter and to my horror, my sweet little helper had dumped almost the entire bottle of black pepper onto the squash. I lost it, and my little boy realized it. All I remember is that the anger and frustration that welled up in me was so great that my husband had to come in and calm me down as I paced the kitchen. I was frantically trying to get over the incident and the fact that we wouldn't be eating squash that evening, which was the only thing I was responsible for preparing! Argh!

Unfortunately, my little Luke saw his mommy get so upset, and he realized I was disappointed in him. Instead of responding with a bit of patience and kindness despite the obvious disillusionment, I let my anger get the best of me. I told my husband to take Luke out as he had caused everything to be ruined. The look of distress in my little boy's eyes is what sticks with me even as I am writing this entry, and his words were simply, "I'm sorry mommy," as he started to cry. He felt the pain of rejection from me, and it is something I never want to bring upon him again.

It is one thing to respond with correction, but it must always be done in love as our Heavenly Father does. In this case, my little lamb probably had no idea he had done anything wrong, as he is still figuring out the world and how it works. I can just imagine his face lighting up as he poured the black pepper all over the squash, thinking he was being mommy's secret helper while I wasn't looking. There's a beautiful picture of God's heart here. God sees us making unwise choices and yet He is so gentle to nudge us back to Himself and His ways. Let us, as mothers, always be God's representation of grace to our children.

Jesus, I know I fall short as a person and a mom. I need you to tear off and chisel away the areas in my heart that contain selfishness, pride, and false security. Make me new once again, and may my children see their mommy being made new each and every day.

Scripture of the Week:

1 Corinthians 13:4-8
Love is patient, love is kind. It does not envy, it does not boast, it is not proud. It does not dishonor others, it is not self-seeking, it is not easily angered, it keeps no record of wrongs. Love does not delight in evil but rejoices with the truth. It always protects, always trusts, always hopes, always perseveres. Love never fails.

Practical Weekly Application:

1. Spend time in *The Bible* and in prayer with God.
2. Pray for God to help you learn from your mistakes and teach you more about His grace this week. Journal about grace that you receive this week in your own life, and then journal about grace that you give to your children and others.

Angry Mama

31. Embracing the Mess

The theme this year for the mom's church group that I am attending is "A Beautiful Mess." I love the paradox! It does seem like an oxymoron to call any mess beautiful, doesn't it? We normally think we need to constantly strive to get out of our "messes" in life in general. Yet, as mothers of young children, there is no escaping the physical messes that occur. If you already have toddlers, you know what I mean. If you don't, you may not have experienced a house turned upside down and inside out by roaming babies, but other areas of your life may seem unorganized or out of sync from what they were before your little one(s) arrived.

Whatever the mess may be, we can all relate to having one or many! I have recently come to the realization that my house will still be messy, no matter what I do in an attempt to keep it relatively clean throughout the day. I still do the "walk around" with my two-year-old and have him help me organize certain areas of our living room or his room, but it seems that after the mess has been seemingly contained, my 14-month-old son comes and displays the hidden clutter once again! By the way, his nickname given by his grandma is "The Destroyer," so messes in my house at this point just happen naturally all day, every day!

Last Sunday was a day to remember. It was a typical morning in many ways, as my husband and I were trying to get ourselves and the boys ready and out the door to attend church. Every Sunday, the goal for me is more or less the same: attempt to get to church on time with the house somewhat in order before we depart. This past Sunday the house was messier than usual, as not even one room felt orderly. The difference came when I decided in my heart to not allow that reality to negatively affect my outlook on the day or to rob me of the joy I could have in the moment. Did this happen of my own doing? It may seem so, but actually I know myself too well, and this was God's pure grace as I surrendered my control of an orderly house over to Him. The next feeling: precious freedom. I was no longer tormented by the nagging voice in my head to clean in order to feel better about myself. No. And frankly, I liked this new and exhilarating perspective, which allowed me to live without regrets at every turn. Literally, as my toddlers can tear apart any room in 10 seconds flat!

Whether you tend to be somewhat of a clean freak like myself, or the opposite side of the spectrum, there is a lesson for all of us here: take the grace and dis the lie. "What lie?" you may ask. I'm talking about the lie that encircles our minds as women and mothers, which tells us we don't measure up, and that somehow we come up short of the "standard." When this lie creeps up in your thoughts and heart, remind yourself that our Heavenly Father loved us before we ever loved Him (1 John 4:19). Furthermore, if your example to your children is to stay on the treadmill of life and continue striving towards goals that may not even be reasonably attainable in a day with little ones running around, what type of mindset are you going to instill in your children? Don't do this to yourself or to your dear little lambs. Life is too short, and as my twin sister Amber says, "Eternity is very long!" If we renew our minds with the eternal and remember that vacuuming can wait another couple of days if need-be, we will free up our spirits and lives to God's sweet divine appointments and leadings that can take place within our home, at the store, or in our own times of intimate communion with God.

Jesus, my life and home seem messy much of the time. Help me to separate physical messes from spiritual ones. I would much rather have a messy home and a freed up spirit that is closely connected with You, my Lord. Give me Your grace to extend to myself when I feel inadequate in keeping up with the messes in my life, and teach me to let go and embrace even the messy seasons that I am living in.

Scripture of the Week:

Matthew 6:19-24
"Do not store up for yourselves treasures on earth, where moths and vermin destroy, and where thieves break in and steal. But store up for yourselves treasures in heaven, where moths and vermin do not destroy, and where thieves do not break in and steal. For where your treasure is, there your heart will be also. The eye is the lamp of the body. If your eyes are healthy, your whole body will be full of light. But if your eyes are unhealthy, your whole body will be full of darkness. If then the light within you is darkness, how great is that darkness! No one can serve two masters. Either you will hate the one and love the other, or you will be devoted to the one and despise the other. You cannot serve both God and money."

Practical Weekly Application:

1. Spend time in *The Bible* and in prayer with God.
2. If you are not used to living with a mess yet because your baby or babies are too small, ask God to show you how you can surrender your grip on this now. If you do live in a "beautiful mess" already, sit down on your couch in the

midst of it and make a list of all the things that are out of place or messy. Then, picture the room in mint condition but with no children in the house. Journal how you would feel if your sweet and precious babies were no longer there to make those messes, and may that spur you on to cherish the inevitable "messes" in your daily life.

Embracing the Mess

32. Defeated

I wish I had written this entry last week, when I felt defeated almost every moment of every day. Instead, I refrained from writing and was in survival mode whenever I had free time, which included taking naps and going to bed extra early.

Interestingly, as I write this entry and attempt to engage in a nostalgic pity party with myself as the guest of honor (or dishonor!), based on last week's events, I am amazed at what I find. I realize that a lot of what "happened" was not earth-shattering or terribly difficult. What was present throughout the entire week, however, was how I processed events, which turned into a pessimistic attitude. I felt incompetent as a mother. I am also expecting baby number three and still in my first trimester. Now yes, my toddler was extra defiant, as he is approaching his third birthday and needed constant discipline and attention. By the time five o'clock rolled around, I was in tears most days and my husband was there to help pick up the pieces of my day and myself that seemed to be in shambles all over our house. I now clearly see that my feeling of defeat had skewed my vision, causing me to perceive every little incident as overwhelming.

Often, there are dangerous lies underlying and perpetuating a feeling of defeat. For one, I believed the lie that I was going to fail, and so no matter what I attempted, it would end in devastation and defeat. I failed to claim God's promises that He desires to give us hope and a future (Jeremiah 29:11). I have to admit that a few thoughtless comments and negative reactions from others in the past few weeks affected me so deeply, that I regarded myself as a completely incapable person and mother. Now, we are all incompetent without Christ, and that is the truth. Yet, once Christ is a part of our daily lives, our victory is already guaranteed, though the battle still needs to be fought. "For when I am weak, then I am strong" (2 Corinthians 12:10). What music to my ears, and wisdom for our souls. Let us not just read it, but claim it and act on those words.

Jesus, You are my competence, my energy, my purpose in life, and my song each day. Without you I have nothing, but if I remain in you I can release the agony of defeat that entangles my thought-life, and press into Your truths for Words of life and light. Thank you that as a mom I can be weak, and YOU will be my strength. Shine in my weaknesses today and may others, including my children, see Your strong arms enfold me.

Scripture of the Week:

Isaiah 49:15-16
Can a mother forget the baby at her breast and have no compassion on the child she has borne? Though she may forget, I will not forget you! See, I have engraved you on the palms of my hands; your walls are ever before me.

Practical Weekly Application:

1. Spend time in *The Bible* and in prayer with God.
2. Write down a lie you have believed about yourself recently. Pray over the Scripture passage for this week and may this be a beginning to dispelling the lie in your heart.

Defeated

33. You're Not Missing Out! Changing Your Perspective...

The friends that I had before I became a mother were one thing, but the friends that I have now as a mother are another. What do I mean? Friends, particularly those who are not parents yet, have one mindset, which is to have fun nights out and get together on a fairly regular basis. I admit that I myself was like this, and was totally clueless to the changes of motherhood until I entered that stage in life.

Once I did become a mom, the harsh reality for me of having to return to work after my first little lamb was less than four months old turned my world on its head. I no longer had the same desires to go out, be in the limelight, or see old friends— unless I could also take my new little bundle with me. He was now my focus, and everything else had to fit in around his schedule and his needs.

I remember being invited out many times after having my first son, and feeling the need to please my friends by joining them. At the same time, I felt uneasy and unready to let go of my new responsibilities of nighttime rituals including bath, books, and nursing. What I do remember is that somehow I had the courage and wisdom to say, "No, I can't go tonight. I really want to be with Luke." I felt somehow that they were disappointed in me, and would feel a personal rejection, no matter how hard I tried to explain what I was experiencing as a new mother. Thankfully, what comforted me in moments when I knew I wanted and had to say NO, was the thought that one day they will understand when they too become a mommy.

Are we missing out on some late nights out with the girls? Yes. Are we able to go out whenever we please? NO. This is the new normal, and this is the life of a mother, a parent, or at least one that truly embraces all the sacrifices and joys that accompany it. You may feel that you are missing out, but have you ever realized what you are gaining? Savor the unrepeatable times of bonding with your child when he/she needs it most, including smiles, giggles, and late-night cuddles with your baby. I hear every mom that is farther down the road echo the message, "One day there will be a longing and aching in your heart to just go back." Now please, hear me clearly. Yes, we will be able to go out and have nights without our babies, but let that be the exception and not the rule, and only when you are ready. In the meantime, don't feel bad about saying "no" to your friends and family, and enjoy when you can say "yes!"

Jesus, it is hard to not be a people-pleaser, especially since I feel the need to connect with others outside of being a mother. Yet, keep me grounded in my role to my children first and foremost, and allow me to highly regard and value it as you do. Thank you for demonstrating to me as my Heavenly Father that time together is necessary to build and nurture a relationship.

Scripture of the Week:

Mark 10:45
For even the Son of Man did not come to be served, but to be serve, and to give his life as a ransom for many.

Practical Weekly Application:

1. Spend time in *The Bible* and in prayer with God.
2. Write down some examples of sacrifice you made this week as a mother. Take time in prayer to talk to God about how you felt and ask for His presence to wash over your spirit, not allowing any lies or attacks from the enemy to take hold in your heart.

You're Not Missing Out! Changing
Your Perspective...

34. Different Seats. Same Flight.

*I*sn't it interesting how God has designed things to work in this world? He has made little babies to grow inside of a mother's tummy to be born, cared for, and to grow up to continue the cycle of rebirth.

I have been having a lot of emotional/tear-jerking moments recently. They are the result of realizing that despite the tired, challenging work that being a mom to young children is, I can't help but remember that it seems like just yesterday I was a new mother, holding my first little bundle and beginning this journey. How ironic that everyone around you seems to be humming the same tune, "Just enjoy these moments, as they grow up so fast." We hear it, but when we are living and breathing diapers, bottles, naptimes, and temper tantrums, can we fathom that one day we too will be repeating that same line to another young mom? Can we comprehend that we too will immensely miss these grueling yet rich days of life with young children? There are only so many days for carefree fun in the sun, cuddles and kisses galore, books read on mommy's lap, sweet and easy laughter, puzzles to accomplish together, and trips to the store for a new toy to light up their eyes and imagination.

As mothers we are all in different seats, but we're on the same flight. There are days in which I seem to gloat in the glory of motherhood, and my perspective is so stuck on loving my little lambs. Other days, survival of the fittest seems to be the underlying yet unspoken motto in our home! At the end of the day, everything is relative. You, as a mother, have gone through, are experiencing, or will pass through uncharted territory that I, as a mother, have never traversed and vice versa. Much of motherhood is universal, but there are those areas determined by the personalities, special needs, and characteristics specific to our own children, family, life experiences, and attitudes. We may all be on the same flight, but be sensitive to the fact that each one is sitting in a different seat, a different place, a different season, and a different stage in the journey. You may be pulling your hair out for a year from frustration in raising a toddler, while I may be praying for wisdom and, if possible, for my little boy to be healed of a scary illness. You may have just had a panic attack after having found permanent marker adorning your toddler's bedroom furniture, and another woman spent that time crying because she found out once again that she isn't pregnant. Can we learn from each other? The more we take our eyes off our own scenarios, we may just awaken to someone else's reality that could inspire us to keep on and live with Christ's endurance.

Jesus, I know that You are the pilot and that no matter how trying the flight can be, I can trust the destination to Your hands. Give me greater vision to see the hurts, joys, and lives of others around me, that I may run the race that I am called to with perseverance, empathy, and compassion.

Scripture of the Week:

2 Corinthians 1:3-4
Praise be to the God and Father of our Lord Jesus Christ, the Father of compassion and the God of all comfort, who comforts us in all our troubles, so that we can comfort those in any trouble with the comfort we ourselves receive from God.

Practical Weekly Application:

1. Spend time in *The Bible* and in prayer with God.
2. Pray over the women and/or fellow mothers in your life who you know are experiencing extra challenges in their lives. Make a date with another mom this week and talk about how her "flight" is currently and how you can best pray for her, and then share about your "flight" so that she in turn can pray for you.

Different Seats. Same Flight.

35. Sweet Sickness!

This winter in my hometown of Buffalo, New York, has been brutally frigid and long! It is hard to be inside all day with two active boys who long to get out all their pent-up energy. I have learned NOT to say, "We are all healthy," because it seems like right after that I am eating my words! That is exactly what happened this past week. I was giving thanks for a few weeks of healthy children and then, almost amusingly, both boys caught a virus. I don't know what's worse—for me (mom) to be sick, or for my boys. Obviously it's hard seeing them uncomfortable, but the upside is I am well enough to take care of them. When everyone is sick we hunker down, call for some help with meals or grocery trips if I can, and just persevere!

So, in the midst of this extraordinarily cold winter, my boys got sick. As moms, those are the days we sometimes wish we could crawl back in bed and have someone else take care of us for a change. On days like this I usually don't tackle laundry or wash many dishes. I also know I won't have time or energy for writing, which is my creative outlet. It is true that sometimes we need to endure, as there are days that are around the clock demanding. On the flipside, let's look through your child's eyes for a moment. Your child may wake up uncomfortable from a fever and know that he/she is in need of mommy's tender care. Despite our lack of energy at times, your child expects that mommy will respond and help make the illness better, or more bearable for the day. Looking back, I have countless memories of such tender care from my mother at any age when I was ill.

A few days ago, one of my little men was quite sick, and he is the one who is usually on the go, nonstop, can't sit still even to read with me for more than a few minutes. As much as it broke my heart to see him sick, it also allowed me to experience wrapping my little boy up in my loving arms for the entire day. My "mover" became my cuddle bug, and the sickness in his body also brought about a sweet togetherness that day. I still don't think there is anything more soothing and healing than the privilege of sensing a little body resting on your own, in utmost tranquility.

Jesus, I want to soak in all the goodness that can come from apparent challenges, including sickness among those in my family. Give me Your set of eyes and a heart of patience. Wrap me up in Your loving arms on those more strenuous days of sickness, in order to see Your sweetness in my babies. I love you.

Scripture of the Week:

Romans 5:1-5

Therefore, since we have been justified through faith, we have peace with God through our Lord Jesus Christ, through whom we have gained access by faith into this grace in which we now stand. And we boast in the hope of the glory of God. Not only so, but we also glory in our sufferings, because we know that suffering produces perseverance; perseverance, character; and character, hope. And hope does not put us to shame, because God's love has been poured out into our hearts through the Holy Spirit, who has been given to us.

Practical Weekly Application:

1. Spend time in *The Bible* and in prayer with God.
2. Take some time to reflect on your life before motherhood compared to your life now. Make a list of similarities and differences. Share your list with another mom in your life and praise God for the challenges as well as the indescribable joys in the midst of it all.

Sweet Sickness!

36. Accident

*I*t was a day I won't ever forget, and a day that in many ways I wish I could. It was the end of March, and my little Luke had come down with the twenty-four-hour stomach bug the day before. My husband and I caught it next. We both were going on almost zero energy while trying to take care of two little boys as well as hosting Jorge's father, who was staying with us on a long-term visit. Just as midafternoon approached, I thought we had been through the worst and were going to come out okay on the other side. My second son was only five-months-old at the time, so when he went down for his nap I decided to go upstairs and attempt to sleep a bit myself. "Finally some solitude and restoration for my aching, broken body," I thought. Well, my blissful sleep was soon interrupted by a scream that pierced through the fibers of my being. It was Luke. Something had happened. I rushed downstairs to find him in my husband's arms weeping, in extreme pain. He had fallen off a spin toy, onto the carpet in our living room. All I knew was that the cry I heard was not a normal one. I tried to take off his shirt, but he jerked his arm back in discomfort. At that point we knew he had to be checked out by a doctor. Unfortunately, my one-year-old had a broken arm—a radial fracture. How could this happen, in our safe living room of all places? I was overwhelmed with guilt, worry, and fear.

I wanted to hide for the next month when I found out he'd have his cast on for at least that long. I had been to the emergency room with my son once before, so even more guilt overcame me as I literally felt as if I couldn't properly protect my own children. I had to realize that no matter what, this was an accident and I had no way of preventing it. I had to forgive myself.

We have to forgive ourselves as mothers for the accidents that have and will take place. Even with the most vigilant eyes, we CAN miss something. Let's admit it, we WILL miss something. If you haven't had any major accidents come along, don't boast or puff up your pride just yet. Motherhood is going to throw you some curve balls, and some of them will hit your precious little ones and send you soaring into a panic. Prepare yourself for this and forgive yourself in advance. Accidents happen. Praise God that His grace always abounds. Give grace to yourself especially in the times where

Satan will urge you otherwise. Even in the so called "accidents" of life, remind yourself that God ordained all things and permitted them to occur in our fallen world. God is in control and will bring good out of our circumstances. Pray for a revelation of His heart and purposes behind the pain.

Jesus, I know accidents happen. As much as I would love to have peace and sheer happiness every day, You remind me that it is in the valleys of life that we grow. Help me to forgive myself and embrace Your purposes even on the hard days when things seem to be falling apart.

Scripture of the Week:

2 Peter 1:2
Grace and peace be yours in abundance through the knowledge of God and of Jesus our Lord.

Practical Weekly Application:

1. Spend time in *The Bible* and in prayer with God.
2. This may seem strange, but make a list of all the mistakes you find yourself making this week. Praise God for the grace He gives you to learn from these mistakes, whether intentional or not. May they serve as a humbling reminder of our need for Him in our lives, and specifically in our mothering. We are not enough, but He sure is.

Accident

37. Personality Differences Among Children

After having my firstborn, I thought I knew how all babies acted. I think one assumes that their first baby mirrors most others, unless you were a mother that had multiples right off the bat, which probably clued you in right away to the astounding differences among your own children!

For starters, let's examine my two boys in the area of reading books, just to give you an idea of the differences among them at this point. My first son, Luke, was turning pages of books at only a few months old in his portable play yard, which made me very proud as a teacher! Between four to six months of age, he loved sitting and reading books on my lap for longer periods. He even started laughing at the same parts of certain books and had books he liked and books he would actually refuse to read as a six-month-old! So, needless to say, he was a pretty early "reader!" By the time he was close to a year he loved sitting with me for literally an hour or more at a time to read. My little bookworm was becoming so bright, and of course I silently patted myself on the back for all his diligent progress.

When Bennett came along, I had no reason to think differently until my reading strategies seemed to not work quite the "magic" they did with my first. He actually never took an interest in books for almost his entire first year! Instead of turning the pages by two months old like Luke, he refused to sit still and pushed all our wonderful books away. I gave him some grace at the beginning, but then I remember feeling frustrated, wondering how I could turn him more into being like Luke somehow. How naive!

Did you see how I saw Luke as "better" just because he has taken to books a lot quicker than Bennett? Let's take a look at the flipside. Bennett was given the nickname "dream baby" by his grandma as soon as he came home from the hospital. For the first four months or more of his life he barely cried at all, and I really mean that! If he was hungry he moaned gracefully and waited patiently. I even told my pediatrician that I felt like I didn't have a real baby in my home this time around. Luke, on the other hand, was what I would term a "normal baby" in the sense that he screamed bloody murder in the night when he needed to be fed. He usually wanted to be held and not laid down in his play yard to "play," and hated car rides, resulting in even more crying.

As you can see now, it's not about which child is better than the other or how we should be molding one to be more like the other. This is the beauty of unique differences among people, and in this case among our own children.

Be careful not to pre-judge your child in a positive or negative way based on your own conceptions or notions of "success." Let us consider how much God would teach us if we could look at the special differences in our children and embrace them fully, nudging them towards God's design and desire for their individual personalities and character above all.

Jesus, give me Your eyes to see my child the way you do—as a unique creation that is meant to bless my life and teach me along the way to seek You more. I desire to build up the distinct personalities and traits that you have bestowed upon my children so that each child becomes the person that You, not I, meant for them to be.

Scriptures of the Week:

Jeremiah 1:5
Before I formed you in the womb I knew you, before you were born I set you apart; I appointed you as a prophet to the nations.

Genesis 1:27
So God created mankind in his own image, in the image of God he created them; male and female he created them.

Practical Weekly Application:

1. Spend time in *The Bible* and in prayer with God.
2. If you have two or more children, make a list of the similarities and differences among them that you have noticed so far. If you have one child, compare him/her to another child or baby that you know and do the same. Pray over these lists and cry out to God for the wisdom you will need to reach your child for who he/she is.

Personality Differences Among Children

38. It's Not About Me!

I had a little "break down" the other day, and I will admit that I am calling it little to make myself feel better!

Okay, so I woke up and felt like I had literally been hit by a train. The short five hours of interrupted sleep that I did get did not seem to suffice. This is mainly because I am expecting my third little blessing and am still in the first trimester survival stage on top of caring for two toddlers. I looked in the mirror on that snowy, bitterly cold morning, and could barely keep my eyes open.

Needless to say, I was resistant to admit that it was a day in which I was physically incapable of taking care of and enjoying time with my boys. I later came to the realization that I should have asked for help from my husband or mother to make it through the day. That was also the day that my older son refused a nap. I felt guilty. Guilty that I couldn't properly care for and have fun with my boys the way I do on most days. Yet, when I looked behind the curtain of guilt that enveloped my heart, I discovered my own selfish pride filling the empty space. Yes, I want to do the best job I can as a mom and take care of my children, but is my motivation simply so that I feel good about it? Or, am I concerned about my children and their future as they take note and are shaped by the character qualities they see in their mommy? If I am brutally honest, I am still thinking of me way too much.

It is twisted, because it can appear as if I am thinking of my children first. But if I really was, I would have asked for help that day. Instead, I chose to give myself the glory for the "hard work" and care that I put in even on a day where my physical body did not want to function. Selfish pride. The world may applaud us and say "well done" for having gotten through it, but if we can reach out our hands to someone else, humble our hearts, and ask for help, the pride we feel as mothers will most likely be revealed as what it truly is: weakness. And that, according to the Bible, is exactly where God wants us—in a state of humble submission.

If we are raising kids with the goal of being wonderful, wholesome, and exemplary mothers, we have still failed miserably in God's sight. It can't be about me. It isn't about me. Yes, I am a huge instrument that God uses to impact my children, but how should I strive towards goodness as a mother? It has everything to do with me decreasing and Him increasing. It is a glorious thing to represent Christ to our children in the role of motherhood. However, clinging to the notion of, "I want to be the best mom I can be," still rings painstakingly of, "It is all about me, as the mom, in the end." So, if our kids fail, is it always our fault? Or if they succeed, is it our "good mothering" that we or others can praise? Our influence matters, but we alone shouldn't eat up all the credit. Only Jesus deserves the glory, so let us constantly remind ourselves and others that He is behind me, and all of the success.

Jesus, the more I see of me the less I like of me. I know You are the reason behind all the blessings, rewards, and successes I have in my life and in my children's lives. Help me to be very intentional about beginning to believe that and to give credit to You when others see Your work in our family.

Scripture of the Week:

John 3:30
He must become greater; I must become less.

Practical Weekly Application:

1. Spend time in *The Bible* and in prayer with God.
2. Ask a friend or family member this week for help. They could come over to babysit for a while so you and your husband can have a date night, or just you go and spend some time by yourself or with a close friend.

It's Not About Me!

39. My Biggest Fears

*I*n just seven more months I will be facing two of my biggest fears—giving birth and then taking care of a newborn! This will be baby number three for us, and you would think I would have or could have conquered some of those scary feelings by now. Well, not really! I think having gone through it twice already has just heightened my awareness to the difficulties and trials that await me once again.

Giving birth is probably an obvious fear for many women, and in my case, I was able to have natural childbirths. So, as miraculous as it was to deliver my babies, it was also a painful process. What I loved was the utter sensation of accomplishment that overcame me, knowing that my body had just undergone a war to get those babies out, and it survived. I survived to tell about it and to hold them in my arms!

With my first little guy, my husband was finishing his studies so he was home a lot and was able to be by my side, helping in my recovery and learning how to care for a newborn. My second newborn experience seemed harder, despite my mother's constant help during those first weeks. This was probably because I already had one child to take care of. When I pondered what was at the root of my "newborn fear," I quickly unraveled the facts: I wanted to be in control. I wanted my own familiar schedule. I wanted to know when I could go to bed and when I would get up. The truth was, all those comforts were and will be stripped away from me once again with the arrival of our third little blessing.

When all the securities we cling to—such as our job, family, or financial reputation—are stripped away, do we have a stable, lasting, and valuable identity? We are on shaky ground, very shaky ground, if we don't build our foundation on Christ as people, as women, and as mothers. The temporary state of panic that seems to enter into my system when my newborn won't sleep on my timetable shows me that I need a more lasting dependence on Our Heavenly Father.

Jesus, thank you for the lessons in humility, our desire to trust in You, and the perseverance that you teach us as mothers. Help me soak up these truths and apply them in deeper ways as I experience being a mom.

Scripture of the Week:

James 1:2-3
Consider it pure joy, my brothers and sisters, whenever you face trials of many kinds, because you know that the testing of your faith produces perseverance.

Practical Weekly Application:

1. Spend time in *The Bible* and in prayer with God.
2. Jot down your top fears as a mother at this stage. Take time to pray over these fears this week and release them back into God's grip, that He might assure you that even if those things come to pass, HE is still in control.

My Biggest Fears

40. Receive

*E*very morning, I seem to have endless time to get ready, eat breakfast, enjoy time with my husband, and pick out the perfect new outfit for an exciting and brand-new day. Did you believe me? Probably not, as I don't know any moms who feel this way!

The truth is, on most days I feel like I am on a treadmill, and some days it is at a speed that is hard to keep up with. I know that my most primitive duties as a mother need to be accomplished first, which include feeding, dressing, and if necessary bathing my little ones. Then, hopefully, I can do the same for myself. Let's admit it, the one thing us mothers need is to be served from time to time.

So, a friend or a family member pops over unexpectedly and brings you a coffee or a hot lunch. Don't let your first reaction be, "You didn't have to do that!" Instead, be honest and tell them just how much it means in the midst of these intense days in which you aren't ever the first priority. Recently, we hit a time where we had more bills coming at us than we had income. It was stressful to feel somehow irresponsible despite our attempts to be careful with our money. We ended up having a lot of home repairs and unexpected expenses, and our decision was to sell one of our cars to cover all the extra costs. No sooner had we put our car up for sale online and found many interested buyers, than had someone in our family heard of our predicament and responded not with pity, but with a tenderhearted and generous response. Our family members decided God had put it on their hearts to cover the costs of all the expenses we had to cover. Do you know what it felt like? It was as if the weight of that burden had been completely taken off our shoulders and we had been set free. What did my husband and I do? We were overwhelmed with gratefulness and praise to God, and we simply said, "Thank you SO much."

Sound familiar? It reminded me of how I felt when I first invited Christ to forgive my sins and be my Savior. He took away all the ugliness and wiped my past, present, and future sins with His blood and sacrifice. In our culture, it is not common to practice receiving. We always feel more comfortable being the "giver," maybe because it somehow feeds our pride and the conception we so desire for others to have of us being self-sufficient. Let's not kid ourselves though. We are all needy people at times, and the sooner we can learn to receive well and gracefully, the sooner we will be able to be an example of Christ in all His humility. Receiving in humility doesn't mean we demand or expect, but rather we pray and graciously accept when offered a gift. The first free gift we need to accept comes from Our Father, and after that anything else will be counted as a double blessing that may be transmitted through another person, but ultimately is coming straight from Him.

Jesus, thank you for the beauty of a humble heart. I want to have a heart that can give generously but that knows how to receive as well. Challenge me this week to say YES to others when I am offered something, and to learn how to enjoy the gift without feeling guilty or ashamed.

Scripture of the Week:

James 1:17
Every good and perfect gift is from above, coming down from the Father of the heavenly lights, who does not change like shifting shadows.

Practical Weekly Application:

1. Spend time in *The Bible* and in prayer with God.
2. Humble yourself to a very vulnerable place this week. The next time someone offers to do something for you, accept it with gratefulness and without excuses. Write down how you felt after having received something you didn't necessarily deserve, but someone graciously offered to you. Enjoy saying "thank you" this week and in the weeks to come, as you learn to joyfully receive.

Receive

41. Creative Cleaning

*I*t takes a lot out of your day just to feed, bathe, clothe, and play with your kids. Having said that, you have to know something about me that perhaps you may find affinity with or perhaps you may think is utterly strange. I love to clean! I find satisfaction in the feeling of a clean and tidy environment, which gives my mind peace and an inner calmness to accomplish other tasks, including my devotions and time that I dedicate to writing. Thankfully, I have found some creative ways to clean around "their schedule," which has served to make for a happier mommy.

So, some of these cleaning tips are not rocket science, and many of you may already be doing this. If you are, I hope that this can affirm your efforts, and spur you on to continue if you have found success in it.

Truthfully, my little lambs were and still are very needy, in my estimation. I can't leave them very long before they need "mommy time," or at least need me to be in the room as they play or read. On countless days I would become frustrated that I didn't end up having a slot of time where I could clean without interruptions. Once I changed my mindset to "clean as I go," things actually started getting cleaned little by little, and my lambs remained content and amused.

How do I "clean as I go?" I am still experimenting every day, but I will give you some practical examples.

First, after breakfast, my boys usually play in the living room. I typically attempt to finish sweeping up the kitchen floor and see how long they can amuse themselves. Once I feel they need mommy, I go in and spend a few minutes reading, doing a puzzle, or playing something else with them. While they are briefly playing together or independently, I can dust the coffee table in the living room, or even clean the front windows or television stand that is almost always covered in fingerprints. At least I can see those things fingerprint free every once in a while!

When we go upstairs and the kids are getting a bath, I take that opportunity to tidy the bathroom. I put out new towels, sterilize the sink and toilet, mop the floor if I am ambitious, and wipe the mirror as we all sing silly songs while they splash in the tub.

My older son helps to clean his own room by putting away his books, stuffed animals, and even tucking in his bed sheets. If you have a child that is at least two years old, he or she can be a great helper with "cleanup time," as you work to tackle every room that you step into and leave it a bit cleaner than when you entered. Playing hide and seek is a great way to tidy an area if your child wants to hide while you count and clean! The best part about cleaning this way is that the more you weave it naturally into your day, the less you feel you need to do when you should be taking a break (a.k.a. naptime/downtime)!

There may be days when even the "clean as you go" method is not sitting well with your kids. What to do? Ditch it for the time being. Play with them, without cleaning at all. Love on them. We should never feel like we have to clean at all times either. Take a break and put your feet up when naptime for the kids rolls around. Your kids, husband, and your own physical body will thank you later.

Who said mommy had to clean all by herself? Although at times it is nice to do without interruptions! We know that our house can get very messy, very quickly, but if we clean a little bit here and there as we go while still enjoying our precious children, how can we lose?

Jesus, thank you for a place to raise my children. I know that having a relaxing and clean home environment is good for our family. I don't desire to be a perfectionist, but I do desire to maintain an orderly home as much as possible.

Scripture of the Week:

Titus 2:3-5
Likewise, teach the older women to be reverent in the way they live, not to be slanderers or addicted to much wine, but to teach what is good. Then they can urge the younger women to love their husbands and children, to be self-controlled and pure, to be busy at home, to be kind, and to be subject to their husbands, so that no one will malign the word of God.

Practical Weekly Application:

1. Spend time in *The Bible* and in prayer with God.
2. Try not focusing on everything that needs to be done in a day this week, but what you can do in each little moment that God gives you throughout your day. Include your children in the tidying process of your home as much as possible this week, and take time to teach them how you do certain tasks that they too are capable of.

Creative Cleaning

42. Self-Consciousness

I didn't wipe his nose well enough. Why is their hair messy AGAIN? Sticky hands for all to touch, great. Did they see that stain on his jacket? Oh no, my friends just witnessed my car full of cookie crumbs! If he throws a tantrum in this place I will be so embarrassed. I forgot to pack an extra snack, and now I am going to look like the worst mom on the planet. Everyone must think my kid never stops crying, bothering, jumping, or misbehaving. [End of internal mental conversation!]

Before we became mothers, we experienced times when we feared what others thought of us. Now that we are mothers, sometimes those thoughts can haunt us even more as there is much more responsibility on our shoulders in the day-to-day of being a mom.

I won't say where this happened, so as not to disclose the identity of the person, but just last week my husband and I and our two boys had an errand to run. Once we arrived at our destination, despite a pretty tense car ride due to cranky little guys on a cold, wintry night, a bit of calm seemed to sweep into the air as we entered the store. To make a long story short, we ran into a family acquaintance and began to chat. Shortly after I shared the exciting news that I was expecting baby number three, our two little ones seemed to hit their breaking point. In addition, this woman had also found out that I was no longer in the workforce as a teacher, and bewilderment, disappointment, and disdain was written all over her face. Her cold and judgmental reaction to our circumstances and decisions hit me. I felt self-conscious, as if I should be ashamed at the path my husband and I have chosen for our children (which includes some financial sacrifices due to mommy being at home). However, then it hit me: there is nothing to defend here. Now, if we were being completely irresponsible with our money and decision-making, that would be one thing. However, why am I allowing self-consciousness and shame to come over me for a very personal dream that I have now fulfilled, which is to be a stay-at-home mom to my kids?

If we allow the thoughts, opinions, habits, or even good intentions of others to dictate our daily lives as moms, self-consciousness may overcome us. Even well-intended advice can make us feel inadequate. We may be overly sensitive to opinions given. Let us ask God for His wisdom in discerning the advice of others, and be kind in our responses.

Jesus, I admit I can be self-conscious about myself and about the way I mother my children. There is so much pressure to be "put-together" and yet I know when I attempt to meet that standard on most days, I still come up short. Give me grace to know it is okay and the wisdom to reject the shame I may feel inside. You are my all in all and YOU, Jesus, ARE enough.

Scripture of the Week:

Galatians 1:10
Am I still trying to win the approval of human beings, or of God? Or am I trying to please people? If I were still trying to please people, I would not be a servant of Christ.

Practical Weekly Application:

1. Spend time in *The Bible* and in prayer with God.
2. Choose this week to see the blessings in disguises that may arise in your family. Write about the challenges you are facing this week or in each particular day, and then list all the blessings that can, could, or will come from them!

Self-Consciousness

43. It's Just Plain Hard Sometimes...No Ifs, Ands, or Buts About It!

*D*o you ever feel frustrated trying to deal with everything difficult that comes into your life? Another unexpected expense for which we were financially unprepared, but I guess it's all going to be "okay." How about those days that seem endless because you feel like nothing you do is appreciated, as your kids seem to just whine louder or more often? But, of course, it is "okay" because in the end it is all somehow "worth it." Is it? Or someone close to you passes away suddenly, and others tell you, "God allowed this for a reason."

Now, I don't think those rationalizations are inherently wrong, but I do believe there is a time to just sit, cry, and admit life can be difficult, overwhelming, and senseless. Let us think, who else thought this way?

If we look in the Bible we find Job who cries out to God in his anguish after having his entire family and estate stripped away from him in a matter of hours—and that means all his children. Can you imagine? He lost all his kids in one day. To put it lightly, Job's response was utterly humane, and he wasn't afraid to let God know there was nothing he necessarily did or didn't do to merit these tragedies in his life. Job cries out to God in Job 30:19-21 saying, "He has cast me into the mire, And I have become like dust and ashes. I cry out to You for help, but You do not answer me; I stand up, and You turn Your attention against me. You have become cruel to me; With the might of Your hand You persecute me."

Second, look at the Psalms where David pours out his broken heart to the Lord. He doesn't try to sugarcoat anything after having committed adultery and then murder in an attempt to cover up his wrongdoing. He writes in Psalm 40:17, "But as for me, I am poor and needy; come quickly to me, O God. You are my help and my deliverer; LORD, do not delay."

Are we comfortable crying out to God and giving ourselves time to mourn certain trials? Or, do we avoid feeling the weight of hardship and instead bury it deep within our hearts where seeds of resentment and bitterness begin to take root and GROW? Yes, seeds will produce a harvest, whether a good one or a foul one. The greatest victories that have ever been won in my life have come while I have been on my knees, in submission to God, being reminded of my inability to understand and comprehend His plan in the chaos.

Maybe in our days as moms we need to stop for five minutes every day and make sure we have time to be honest with Our Heavenly Father about what has affected us in the past week, day, or even minutes! If we never cry out to God about our fears, hurts, struggles, burdens, or worries, who are we crying out to? Don't pick up the telephone this time. Go directly to Your Father with this one. Make it a habit to seek Him first and be brutally honest about your feelings with Him. Whatever it is, it's nothing that He doesn't know, so don't be afraid to put words to it and say it aloud because He already recognizes what is in your heart. The bonding comes when you spend that time with Him in prayer, communing with Your Father.

Dear God, You are my source. Without you this plant (me) will wither and die, so why do I think I can go for long stretches without Your everlasting light and water in my life? I want to be more real with you this week, and in this honesty I pray that You would provide healing for the broken places in my life.

Scripture of the Week:

Psalm 18:1-3
For the director of music. Of David the servant of the LORD. He sang to the LORD the words of this song when the LORD delivered him from the hand of all his enemies and from the hand of Saul. He said: I love you, LORD, my strength. The LORD is my rock, my fortress and my deliverer; my God is my rock, in whom I take refuge, my shield and the horn of my salvation, my stronghold. I called to the LORD, who is worthy of praise, and I have been saved from my enemies.

Practical Weekly Application:

1. Spend time in *The Bible* and in prayer with God.
2. Take the first five to ten minutes of naptime for your kids or bedtime at night to go before the Lord and tell him how you feel each day this week. Be real and just enjoy communing with God.

It's Just Plain Hard Sometimes...No Ifs, Ands, or Buts About It!

44. Sing Mama, Sing

My oldest lamb Luke was being tucked into bed a few nights ago by my husband. The coast was clear and he appeared to be "down for the count" that night, when suddenly a faint and tiny voice could be heard in our hallway and traveled down the stairs. Luke was up, and he needed his mama. I reluctantly went into his room and sat next to his bed.

I began singing different songs quietly over him, which he usually enjoys, but this night was extra special. Luke heard my voice and responded, "Sing mama, sing," whenever my tone grew quieter and weaker as I tried to wean him to sleep with my lullabies. He made me feel like I was a Hollywood star, and that he couldn't get enough! Well, what he couldn't get enough of was his mama's voice, his mama's presence, and ultimately his mama's love towards him. In those three words my day was wrapped up with a precious bow and given back to me as a priceless gift, undeservingly. It had actually been a day with numerous trials from that same little boy, Luke, who is challenging me with his "No mommy" and temper tantrums on a daily basis. But nothing mattered now, because all was forgiven and made well once again as I loved on my little one in spite of all the ups and downs of our day.

Let's let our Heavenly Father's voice sing over us this week in particular. We can't possibly tackle all the obstacles that will come our way, so let the soothing song from His Words in Scripture and in times of personal prayer warm your heart with His faithful promises to never leave us nor forsake us, and to always work for the good of those who are called by His name. Release. Listen. Hear Him singing.

Scripture of the Week:

Zephaniah 3:17
The LORD your God is with you, the Mighty Warrior who saves. He will take great delight in you; in his love he will no longer rebuke you, but will rejoice over you with singing.

Practical Weekly Application:

1. Spend time in *The Bible* and in prayer with God.
2. Make sure to really dig into the Word this week and allow God to speak to you as His precious child. Just as you long to spend time with your child/children, give that privilege to God and stop the busyness around you each day for a short time to make it happen. Journal the verses that God lays on your heart, and the thoughts He puts in your heart and mind this week.

Sing Mama, Sing

45. Encourage One Another

*L*ast night was the first snowfall. The weather is starting to change and Thanksgiving will be here soon. My younger sister, who is also a mother now, and my mom and I decided to meet up at the mall for a change of scenery. My two boys were content in the cute play area, climbing and sliding down the big cars, trucks, and tires. Nearby, the antique carousel played cheerful songs as children waited their turn to choose a colorful animal to spin around on. Just beyond, Santa's station was already set up with two festive elves waiting to snap photos of children curled up on Santa's knee with twinkling Christmas trees in the background.

We decided to walk down to watch the animated Christmas bears that entertain every December with carols and jingles. Today's trip to the mall was filled with so much beauty and pleasure to cause little ones to wonder.

After walking the mall and letting the boys go on one more carousel ride before heading out, I saw a familiar face. It was someone that on occasion I played with as a child. She was now a mother just like me.

I wanted to talk to her right away, but I hesitated. I immediately told my mom, who was already helping to get my tired boys bundled up in their wintry gear to go out to the car. She said to me, "Let's be friendly."

We struck up a conversation with her about her little baby, only five months old. I asked her if she was a part of a mom's group and she said no, so I invited her to one that I attend and gave her my phone number. I was surprised at how appreciative and interested she was in hearing about that, and about running into me.

In the hustle and bustle of the holidays and even just the day-to-day busyness, forgetting what is most important is a trap we all can and probably have fallen into. The beauty and wonder that children feel in this time is precious, but we can have that same wonder and awe of God when we see how He can uniquely and purposefully place people in our paths that might minister to us and to whom we can minister.

Being a mother requires energy, attention, drive, love, patience, and much more. It means that for a short trip to the mall, I may pack snacks, a lunch, fill water bottles, a wet washcloth for dirty hands, and of course diapers and an extra change of clothes "just in case!" Our worlds can seem very small and insignificant if we confine ourselves to viewing our life as an isolated entity. We may have done our duty washing the hands, runny noses, and changing the dirty diapers of our children, but did we bother to notice or reach out to the possible lonely mom attempting to do the same? My prayer is that Jesus changes my vision, so that when I only see my kids and I at a mall food court, I am encouraged to stop and ask for more sensitivity to notice the others around me. With two very antsy little boys waiting by my side, I couldn't chat long with the mom I ran into, but the very brief conversation was meaningful and intentional.

God, I need to be outward focused even as a mom. Help me to take care of my babies well and yet still have Your heart for moms out there who need a friend, and ultimately may need You in their lives. Thank you for the wonder of Christmas, in which You thought of us first and sent your Son to live among us. We love you, Jesus.

Scripture of the Week:

Ephesians 2:10
For we are God's handiwork, created in Christ Jesus to do good works, which God prepared in advance for us to do.

Practical Weekly Application:

1. Spend time in *The Bible* and in prayer with God.
2. Ask God to sensitize your heart this week to the needs of others around you. Pray for boldness so that you can respond to His leading. Make sure to journal about any opportunities God puts in your path as a testimony to His faithfulness when we make ourselves available for His service!

Encourage One Another

46. Unexpected Encounters

oday there is a huge blizzard here in Buffalo, and I somehow managed to briefly get out and zip over to the dentist's office while my mom came and watched my boys. Now, as I sit back at home typing in the middle of the day and sipping hot chocolate (I had to tell you that because it almost never happens!), my husband is out shoveling. Our driveway has accumulated at least six inches or more of snow within the past six hours.

You would have never guessed, but at this time yesterday I was out taking a stroll around the block with my boys in fifty-degree weather, extremely warm for this particular Buffalo winter. Earlier in the day we ended up going to a park that is located right around the corner from our home. As we approached, I saw two other small children playing there, despite all the ice and small piles of snow that had not fully melted. I noticed a slender, petite mom as we got closer, and seeing her there gave me the courage to let my two little ones out on this semi-wintry playground to hope or pretend that summer was here that day!

The mom and I struck up a conversation pretty quickly, and I learned that she is, as of last week, a stay-at-home mom now as a result of an unexpected job loss. She also mentioned her recent divorce, and how shocking it was for her, her family, and friends. She is years younger than I am, and is now a single mom with three small children. I invited her to a Christian mom's group that I attend, and she accepted the invitation. She said everyone tells her, "There is a reason for why this is happening, and why you lost your job." I told her, "God has a plan for this." She said she wasn't raised to be religious, but that she is very conservative. I listened. Our conversation casually continued as we shared brief labor stories and other random baby moments while floating from slides to swings to climbing bars with our little ones. Before leaving, I got her number and told her I would give her a call to remind her about the next mom's gathering. We parted ways and I called her later that day just to say hi.

Unexpected encounters. I can't tell you how many moms I have met at that playground and struck up similar conversations with. It is amazing how much we need each other as people, women, mothers, and friends. The moms that I meet don't know me at all, but somehow we bond over motherhood together. This is vital: Are we capitalizing on motherhood as a ministry opportunity, or so caught up in it that we can't see past our own seemingly cyclical days? Intentionality is so key. I know how hard sleepless nights and endlessly tiring days can be as a mom, and our first ministry is our home. Yet, if you go to a park or somewhere outside your house, just start by praying for the people who you will meet on your way. Maybe striking up a conversation scares you, but you can always start by letting the other mom know how cute, adorable, or handsome her kids are. I always feel special when someone says that, even a stranger! Pray for boldness if this doesn't come easy or natural, because God is calling us all to something bigger than just what is comfortable and routine for us. The moment you realize that your own life, marriage, children, and family as a whole is on display to ultimately represent Christ and lead others to Him, it will be hard to stay silent.

Jesus, your heart is for the lost and dying of this world. Help me to see others as destitute, just as I once was, without your love and presence in our lives. I want to be ready to reach out and proclaim your name both directly (with words) and indirectly (with my life). Praise You God for using broken old me to do Your great and mighty work here on earth.

Scripture of the Week:

Romans 1:16
For I am not ashamed of the gospel, because it is the power of God that brings salvation to everyone who believes: first to the Jew, then to the Gentile.

Practical Weekly Application:

1. Spend time in *The Bible* and in prayer with God.
2. Ask God to give you some unexpected encounters this week. Pray for boldness, as it will take God's sensitized heart in you as well as initiative to take the first step. Journal about the encounters you have and how God worked in and through them!

Unexpected Encounters

47. Those First Days as a Mom...

*I*t's crazy looking back at my first few days as a new mom to our oldest son. I had no idea what I was doing!

I'll never forget those doctor appointments right after giving birth to check the baby's weight and make sure he was gaining enough, particularly because I was nursing and had a very rough go of it. The car rides to and from seemed like an eternity, as I still didn't feel quite comfortable having my little bundle in the car seat and out of my arms, and he wasn't too fond of car rides either. Once we got in I remember feeling exhaustion mixed with adrenaline, with the exhaustion winning the battle. I looked around and saw other mothers there with their children who seemed to become toddlers overnight, and I wondered when I would be there and out of this sleep-deprived state!

Across the room, I noticed a mother checking out with her two young toddlers. She held her youngest, a boy, in her arms, and proudly shared with the staff that she was still successfully breastfeeding him at two years old. Listening to her made me feel like a failure before I had even begun my journey, and I didn't know what standard to live up to now. As I was contemplating, suddenly I heard his name, "Luke Torres," and I realized it was our turn.

Perhaps there is the lesson. When it is our "turn" at motherhood, what standard have we placed on ourselves? Is it reasonable? Unreasonable? Too lenient? Far too lofty? Being a mom does come with so much responsibility, but if there is no grace involved we will soon be down for the count. I realized at that very first doctor's appointment a few things that I wasn't doing correctly, and it devastated me to the point of tears. I felt an array of emotions: fear, failure, depression, worry, doubt, and utter inability. I knew I was down, but I didn't want to stay there for long.

Our Savior can pick us up, dust us off, and wrap us up in His loving arms to brush away those regretful yet unintended mistakes and learning experiences we all have and will go through as mommas. Remember, Our God is intentional and makes no mistakes, so the fact that you are alive and are a mother yourself is another reminder that you were planned, given this precious baby, and loved beyond your imagination.

Jesus, give me realistic, practical, and godly expectations to have of myself as a mom. When I feel failure creep its way in, remind me that mistakes are Your way of teaching me and molding me in life and in motherhood.

Scripture of the Week:

1 Peter 5:6-7
Humble yourselves, therefore, under God's mighty hand, that he may lift you up in due time. Cast all your anxiety on him because he cares for you.

Practical Weekly Application:

1. Spend time in *The Bible* and in prayer with God.
2. Start by writing down a short list of things you feel a wonderful mother would do or possess as character qualities. Now, write down some expectations of yourself that have run through your heart/mind this week that are unreasonable, and then turn them into reasonable expectations that are attainable with God's help.

Those First Days as a Mom...

48. Change it Up!

I don't know if it is just a "me thing," but I guess I do know some other people who have expressed similar tendencies regarding what I am about to share. Bottom line: I personally can't take the same old, same old for too long, at all!

As a mom, life is "cyclical" enough. Yes, it does have its share of unpredictability in the way of accidents, unexpected sleep deprivation on certain nights, etc. (Fun, wow!) However, when another holiday or season comes along or is approaching, I definitely get giddy inside. Why? Well, not just to celebrate the actual occasion, but because I know that I can redecorate the house. That always leaves me with a rejuvenated feeling, as the positive change in our environment creates a new and fresh atmosphere for my children to think, play, and learn.

If you haven't tried this, take a random day when you are tired of the way things look in your living room and change some things around. It's amazing how moving the coffee table from one side of the room to the other has a way of making me feel like I just remodeled my entire living room!

Another way to get out of the same old, same old rut is to spice things up in the kitchen. We probably all get to a point where we become bored with the familiar recipes we have come to so easily depend on. When I am fed up with my food choices (pun intended!), I try to make a goal of learning to make one new recipe or meal each week. I haven't done this yet, but why not recipe swap with some close friends? That way you are more likely to prepare something that you know you may like, knowing your close friends have enjoyed that particular meal. Many hands make light work! In this case, more good recipes make meal preparation and cooking more simple and exciting.

Lastly, I have two active boys. I learned a long time ago that a break in the routine for children can be just as crucial to having a routine! How can you "break" your routine? One way could be by infusing new activities into your days. If you have children who are able to do simple activities, get out some art supplies and make something with them based on an upcoming holiday, season, or important event. It always helps to have a "model" to look at before you begin, so your child/children know what they are trying to create with your guidance. It won't take too much time on your part, as long as you KEEP IT SIMPLE, because you want your children to be doing the majority of the project, not you! One example of something I have done is writing a letter of the alphabet big enough to take up the whole piece of paper. For spring I did the letter "S" with the words, "is for Spring" below it. Have your child take markers, paint, cotton balls, glitter, cereal, stickers, or anything else you can think of that would work, and decorate the letter S with it. They will love trying something new, and you'll have a few special moments of bonding and connection with them as they are learning.

Jesus, thank you for the gift of creativity that enables me to bring healthy changes into our family's life. Allow our times together as a family to be memorable.

Scripture of the Week:

Colossians 3:23
Whatever you do, work at it with all your heart, as working for the Lord and not for human masters, since you know that you will receive an inheritance from the Lord as a reward. It is the Lord Christ you are serving.

Practical Weekly Application:

1. Spend time in *The Bible* and in prayer with God.
2. Change it up this week! Get a new recipe from a friend, try moving some furniture around, or give the kids a change of scenery or a new activity to dive into. You should all feel a bit refreshed and rejuvenated to continue accomplishing His purposes in the day–to-day with some small changes!

Change it Up!

49. My Baby is Eligible for Preschool?

I t hit me when I actually made the phone call to a local preschool inquiring about pricing and schedules. Time really does fly by. How did my innocent, helpless newborn already transform into an intelligent, active, silly little boy? He will be three in a little over a month. I honestly can't believe it. The moments over the course of his short lifetime have been a mixture of sweetness, pain, pleasure, and challenge. How much this little man has changed me, through his presence in our home and my recognition of my weakness before God to do this job on my own.

We are not positive we will be sending our little three-year-old to preschool. Either way, the transition to more and more independence is inevitable and healthy for children to experience. I am not at the point of feeling anxious to have more "time to myself" as the motivation for preschool attendance, and am actually more concerned with him being away from home and how he will perceive the world without me by his side. Yes, in those words I just wrote you can see my struggle—letting go is hard, and yet change is inescapable.

Maybe you already have kids in preschool or school, have chosen to homeschool, or are still waiting, like me, for that day to come. Change can be a very good and positive thing, but it is usually not fully embraced by most. If you are like me, nostalgia can hold its slimy grip over your emotional well-being and actually cause fear to ruin the elation that would otherwise come with life's progressive transitions.

Well, I may be emotional and nostalgic, but I don't want that to cloud the clarity of taking hold and fully living in the stage of life that my child is now traversing. Instead, I may need to let my tears over the beauty of the past intertwine with the blessing of the present: God's greatness reflected in tiny miracles. My child is a miracle to behold, and he or she needs mommy to be rejoicing over him or her in every season of life. Each stage has its challenges and rewards, such as newborn madness coinciding with silent slumber, terrible two tantrums accompanying tender "I love you's," and now possible preschool outings hopefully coupled with loving cuddles once back in mommy's arms.

As you face transitions in life concerning motherhood, relationships, and other areas, are you dreading the changes? Try to embrace these adventures and surrender the outcomes to God, Our Heavenly Father.

Jesus, I don't want to go through transitions without You. Thank you for your faithful Hand to lead me through the changes that I am and will experience. Let me reflect on your past faithfulness to encourage my future devotion to You in these areas of change where doubt can cast its dark shadow. Great is Your faithfulness unto me!

Scripture of the Week:

Genesis 12:1-3

The LORD had said to Abram, "Go from your country, your people and your father's household to the land I will show you. I will make you into a great nation, and I will bless you; I will make your name great, and you will be a blessing. I will bless those who bless you, and whoever curses you I will curse; and all peoples on earth will be blessed through you."

Practical Weekly Application:

1. Spend time in *The Bible* and in prayer with God.
2. Think upon a few transitions you have gone through recently in your time with God, professional experience, or social circle. Pray over your future transitions, things you may not even foresee, and ask for God's vision and help in leading your family closer to God's heart.

My Baby is Eligible for Preschool?

50. Keep Your Circle Open

*L*ife is cyclical in many senses. It begins with helpless babes, ends with old age and frailty to those who make it to that point, and then begins again with another precious miracle for the next generation to behold. We are used to the pattern, but are awakened to its reality when we experience the joy of a new birth, or the pain and suffering of a loss.

As you go through seasons of tragedy and blessing, be reminded that the circle of those around you should be ever growing. Some relationships will endure, while others may grow more distant for various reasons. The key is to never close your circle until God takes you home to glory. What do I mean? Avoid the tendency to think you have "enough friends" or "enough on your plate," and can't possibly befriend another soul. The most amazing friendships in my life right now have come from intentional action on my part to initiate a conversation. I have been blessed beyond measure from them! I could have said, "I have two close sisters and a handful of solid special friendships. I am set and satisfied, no more room." Did Jesus model that? He never stopped seeking and serving those around Him.

Your children desire your affections, your time, and your sweet presence in their lives. Make sure they are in the center of your circle each day. If you work, pray for coworkers. If you stay at home, pray for opportunities in your day. Our circles of fellowship are living testimonies that Jesus is present in our hearts and desires to accomplish His will through us.

Jesus, expand my circle beyond my human conception of capability. Stretch me to model after your example, one that always seeks to serve, include, and bless others.

Scripture of the Week:

Luke 10:27
He answered, "Love the Lord your God with all your heart and with all your soul and with all your strength and with all your mind"; and "Love your neighbor as yourself."

Practical Weekly Application:

1. Spend time in *The Bible* and in prayer with God.
2. Open up your circle this week. Invite someone new into your home and into your life. It could be someone you meet informally, someone you have seen but have never talked to at church, or simply someone you have known but have never intentionally gotten to really know. Enjoy expanding your circle, and pray that God would use it to further His kingdom!

Keep Your Circle Open

51. Why?

id you ever wonder why God allowed it to be so difficult for a mom to be a mom? I guess it started back in Genesis, when Adam and Eve disobeyed and thus the curse was unleashed, which meant men would have to work and labor for food, and women would have great pains in childbirth. For the sake of argument, I think we got the shorter end of the "curse stick"!

So, why did God have to allow pregnancy in its entirety to take around nine months? It seems that after I survive the sacrifice of having a living being take over my body, the true sacrifice begins at birth when I am forever linked to my baby.

To give a simple answer, beauty arises from ashes. Genesis says that God formed us out of the ground's dust, which simultaneously reminds me of life's frailty and wonder. In our brokenness, the loveliness of Jesus breaks forth. It may seem like a paradox to us, but Christ reminds us in the Bible that when we are weak, He is strong.

Just as we are puzzled by the way God has set up and orchestrated the miracle of life, we may also find ourselves questioning the why's in our own lives. Some of my own why questions throughout life have been as follows: Why can't I have a stable job? Why was I born here, in this country, with my particular family? Why can't my husband find work? Why does God allow others to go through hardship such as extreme poverty, despicable abuse, and violent deaths, while many of us seem to be "spared?"

Why? These are questions that can shake us to the core. They can deepen our relationship with God if we depend and trust in Him regardless of having all the answers now, or they can destroy our confidence in Christ if we define who He is merely by what happens in this world. John 16:33 states, "In this world you will have trouble, but take heart, I have overcome the world." The Bible also reminds us in Romans 8:28 that, "God works all things together for good for those who love Him and are called according to His purposes."

Are you living in a pit of why's? Don't stay there. Jesus is the only one who will ever know all the answers to the unexplainable "why's" in our lives. Focus on his past, present, and future victories and faithfulness. Continue praying through the harder why's you will face or become aware of in the lives of others. The One who promised us an eternal life with Him if we simply accept His grace in our lives IS faithful, and one day "He will wipe every tear from their eyes. There will be no more death or mourning or crying or pain, for the old order of things has passed away" (Revelation 21:4). This is God's heart for us. Do you believe it?

Scripture of the Week:

Isaiah 44:7
Who then is like me? Let him proclaim it. Let him declare and lay out before me what has happened since I established my ancient people, and what is yet to come—yes, let them foretell what will come.

Practical Weekly Application:

1. Spend time in *The Bible* and in prayer with God.
2. Write down your scary "why" questions, those that have been haunting you for a while or those that have just recently arisen in your life or in the lives of loved ones. Dig into God's Word this week and pray over the scripture passage listed here. Ask God to instill faith, peace, and joy in your heart and life in place of doubt and isolation from God. Claim HIS victory over the "unanswered" why's. He is faithful.

Why?

52. Imitators

Parks seem to be the places where I spend most of my time these days. A little girl no older than six was there with her lifelike baby doll wrapped tightly in her arms as she climbed up the playground stairs and glided down slides. I watched her as she placed her beloved dolly in the baby swing and pushed her little bundle just like a grown-up mommy would. As she walked away I marveled that she carried her baby doll perfectly balanced on her hip, just like I do when I carry my boys. Imitating.

This little girl gave me a picture of my own heart. It seeks to imitate someone that I admire and desire to be like. Our Heavenly Father calls us to be imitators of Christ, so closely identified with Him that the world would see Christ when they look upon our lives. Now that is a high calling! It may seem that such imitation is impossible, but nevertheless we are called to it.

I don't want my children to look at their mommy and see only a well-intentioned yet sinful person. I truly pray that they would see Christ Himself. I need to surrender my bad attitudes, moodiness, overreactions, and selfishness. Imitate Jesus, and your precious children will grow to naturally imitate Him as well.

Jesus, you are the only One worthy of imitating. Increase in me, so that I may decrease. May this be true in the lives of my children as well.

Scripture of the Week:

Ephesians 5:1
Be imitators of God, therefore, as dearly loved children.

Practical Weekly Application:

1. Spend time in *The Bible* and in prayer with God.
2. Press into knowing Christ this week through more quiet time with Him. Cry out for His power and passion to be present in your heart, so that you aren't leaning on your human strength, but rather on His mighty hand to open doors.

Imitators

A Closing Prayer

I am blessed. Jesus, You are the giver of these beautiful treasures, my children! May you give me wisdom to raise them to know and serve You in the short window of time I have to regularly influence them. Amen.

Endnotes

New International Version. Biblica, 2011.
BibleGateway.com,www.biblegateway.com/versions/New-International-Version-NIV-Bible/#booklist.

77194006R00093

Made in the USA
Middletown, DE
22 June 2018